Beginner

+

Intermediate Guide to Pattern Fitting and Alteration

Table of Contents

Beginner's Guide to Pattern Fitting and Alteration

Introduction

I have a small fitting and alteration shop in New York and I am always swamped with work. From store opening to closing time, customers would come in and out. Weekends are particularly busy as the busy people of New York could only squeeze a free Saturday afternoon for an alteration. I even have standing orders three to six months in advance. Orders range from minor trouser length adjustments and fixing loose seams to major size readjustment and pattern modification. I don't think there will ever be a downtime for fitting and alterations as clothes are an essential part of our lives.

In my line of work, there are two moments in the alteration experience I enjoy the most. The first is hearing the reason for the customer's concern for alteration. I like talking with customers and how they relate with their clothes. When I was starting out, I would interact with them in a straightforward manner. I would simply ask them, "So, what do you want me to do?" and they would proceed to telling me how they want to add an extra pocket or trim the shirt edges. Customers were mostly in control, telling me what exactly they wanted me to do with their clothes. I was simply the alterations tailor: cutting and sewing according to my customer's specifications.

The more I grew in this business, the greater I felt I wanted to have a more active relationship with my customers. I began to have a regular set of customers and I felt bored with the routine of just executing commands. Instead of asking them what exactly they want me to do, I asked them, "With these clothes, what look do you want?" At first customers were startled with my question. They expected me just to be more technical and business-like. That opening would have them really thinking for some time but that question opened up a lot of conversations on people's thoughts on clothes and on how they want to look in general.

Some of the replies were quite interesting to hear.

"I want to look thinner."

"I want to make my hips look smaller."

"I want to emphasize my shoulders."

I took these replies and began customizing their clothes according to the look they want. This was such a refreshing change from the technical approach I was using with alterations. When I know what people want to look like, I can recommend certain alterations that will make my customers feel better about their clothes. It was also a teaching moment for me when I heard their projected look. For example, a client would like to make me trim her trousers just below the knee level. When I asked her what look she was aiming for, she said "I want to look taller." In principle, I agree that shortening the pants can make you look taller. But the length she wanted to go for will not really make her taller. In fact, it would even emphasize her short stature by exposing her entire leg. I recommended that we cut the trousers on the shin area, between the knee and the heel. We could even extend it only until above the heel. In this way, the illusion of long legs can be preserved. She had a look in mind, but her principles of design did not match that. It was a complete change for me, moving from a simple technical tailor to a proactive design collaborator.

There were other standout replies with my initial question. It was such a powerful question that people began opening up about their own lives. A simple question about clothes and looks could easily evolve into a conversation about how they feel about their body or the stress they feel from work. Some of the memorable answers were:

"I want to be able to wear my old clothes from ten years ago. These have a special memory for me, but I just can't fit into them with my current size."

"I want to look confident in my clothes. My bosses are critical of everything and I want to project an image of strength."

"I want to look beautiful. I feel I'm too fat and people around me are staring. I want to feel good about myself."

These anecdotes really touch my heart and make me realize how valuable my work is as a tailor. We may think that fitting and alteration is a simple cutting and trimming of clothes, but we are mistaken. When we are able to make clothes properly fit people, they feel better about themselves. When clothes emphasize the best part of people, customers feel a lot more confident about themselves. When trousers or dresses are able to hide unwanted contours, clients feel more secure about interacting with others. In our own way, fitting and alterations can make people feel beautiful and good about themselves.

I relish the second best moment in my alteration experience: the moment of fitting the new clothes. Usually, people pick up their altered clothes from the shop and try them on at homes. I encourage a lot of my customers to try it on in the shop and then we can make the necessary changes.

This saves a lot of time especially when customers have extra alterations they want to make.I really look forward to seeing them look at the mirror in their newly-altered clothes. The smile on their faces and the confidence they exude as they parade their clothes around the shop is priceless. When alterations uplift people's moods and make them appreciate their own bodies, I feel that I have made a real difference.

This book is written to extend my humble fitting and alterations shop to your home. I really want to share that joy of making clothes work for people to everyone who appreciates and values these articles of clothing. I want to emphasize that everyone has that capacity to alter their own clothes. I have designed this book to be technically relevant to both beginners and those already familiar with the tailoring process. Each lesson is beautifully illustrated so that you will have a good visual that shows what I am talking about. Whether you are altering clothes as a hobby or for your established business, there is something new for you to learn in this book.

I want to make this book more interactive than other pattern-making books. I will describe general principles of design and the how-to for basic pattern fitting and alteration. I have designed each chapter as a mini-project for you to do. Don't just read this book as a leisurely, sit-down read. I envision that you have this book on your work table, and that you are reading the instructions as you are actually making your own clothes. With this book on the table and your hands on scissors and textile, we will accomplish projects and make the learnings really stick. The more clothes you work with, the more precise and accurate your alteration and fitting will be. Don't move too quickly through the projects until you have mastered each. This is not a race to finish the book in a day. Absorb what you can and then practice directly on real clothes. You will get better clothes after clothes, lesson after lesson.

These lessons are culled from my years of alterations and fittings. I will introduce you to basic patterns and fittings. I will also let you in on tricks and hacks I have learned along the way. Some people need to go to fashion school in order to sew and design well. I believe that any who is willing to take up tailoring seriously can learn from anywhere. With my guidance, you will be more confident in your pattern making and even in deciding how clothes fit people well.

I think that as long as people are growing, there is a need for alterations and fitting. People grow tall, get bigger, lose a few pounds, and develop more in some areas, all of which make them beautiful as they are. People develop in all sorts of proportions, which clothes manufacturers don't pay attention to. There are standard sizes like small, medium, large, XXXL: each person is different. The same person now will not be the same size or proportion ten, twenty years from now. Clothes don't grow with people. It is tempting to just buy new ones that fit your current size. A more practical approach is simply to alter your clothes to match your body size at the moment. With a good grasp of basic measuring, sewing and cutting, you will be able to continue using your clothes to fit you in whatever age or context you may be in. By altering and fitting clothes, you extend the lifetime of clothes and help people save money. When you begin to understand the beauty of design, you can transform old clothes into new ones, consequently transforming the person wearing them. Let this book be your guide, accompanying you to your journey as a great tailor and an instrument of transformation.

So what look do you want? Let the journey begin!

Chapter One:
Tools, Equipment and Accessories

I first bought my first set of sewing tools from a tool shop downtown. I remember starting with a tape measure, some scissors, thread and pins. My grandmother was very enthusiastic about my sewing so she gave me a box of colored thread I could use. To this day, I still keep that box with me, now filled with all sorts of pins, thimbles, buttons and a lot of good memories of my grandmother. From that initial set, I began to gather more materials as my shop grew. Each material I got had a memory and a story. Sewing materials grow with you through time.

All alterations must start with your basic tools. You must know the basic tools, equipment and accessories that are needed for you to be able to alter and fit clothes. Most of these materials are accessible and affordable. If you want to continue doing alterations for a long time or if you are thinking of turning your hobby into a full-fledged business, I recommend that you invest in quality materials. Some of my tools have been around for many, many years. If you switch too much between old and new tools, some alteration changes may occur. Hence, make sure that you have the right quality materials before you begin. There are five major categories of alteration tools: measuring, marking, cutting, sewing and accessories. I will be explaining the tools in each category. It may not be enough to just have one tool from each category as there are particular uses for each. Read through the descriptions and see if you will need these tools for your particular needs. For those who are planning to go professional, it is essential that you have all these tools at your disposal. Take in all the tools first before buying them. It is frustrating to keep on returning to the supply store if you don't have all your materials ready at hand. I will mark tools which I think are essential for beginners and those they can postpone until they have mastered the basics.

Measuring Tools

There are four tools which are needed to help you measure sizes. Each tool has a particular function that is more appropriate for particular situations. You need to have an accurate measurement both of the client and of the clothes to be altered. Problems arise when the measurement is off by even a few inches. Some tailors allow allowances in measurements to accommodate movement or possible changes in the client's body size. Make sure to note how to use each measuring tool.

Tape Measure

This is the most essential measuring tool you can have in your supply. Some tailors actually only use the tape measure for everything. But this is inaccurate. The tape measure serves a particular purpose, and that is to measure uneven surfaces. This is particularly indispensable when you are taking body measurements. The flexibility of the tape allows you to cover proportions accurately. You can also use the tape measure for patterns or textile when they are laid on uneven surfaces.

Most tape measures use the inch and metric systems. There are measures which place them both on the same side or on either side. This is good if you want to be as accurate as possible. You have to remember what measuring system you used: things can go awfully wrong when you measured in inches and recorded in centimeters. To avoid this error, use only one system of measurement as much as possible. Label all your measurements so that you don't get confused.

It is also worthwhile to compare the measuring systems. As I have said, try to stick with one system only. If there are cases when you need to switch, you have to know how the units are converted to each other.

Converting FROM	Is EQUAL to
1 inch	2.54 cm
0.4 inches	1 cm
1 feet	12 inches
1 yard	91.44 cm
0.01 yards	1 cm
1 inch	0.28 yards
36 inches	1 yard
1 mm	0.1 cm

When taking body measurements, there are fourteen measurements you need to obtain:

- neck

- bust

- waist

- hips

- front waist length

- back waist length

- arm

- shoulder

- knee

- calf

- instep

- side length to knee

- side length

- crotch

We will discuss how to take measurements for the different projects in the succeeding lessons. It is important for you to remember that the tape measure must accurately record these.

Measuring tapes can be made of fiberglass or cloth. There are those that come with an automatic recoiler and can be made to hold its position like a metal ruler. You need to take care of your measuring tape because they are very prone to damage. You will be using them on a number of surfaces repeatedly and the stretching process can distort tape and therefore the actual measurement. The material can also be frayed or damaged on the edges. Be careful also when you use the fiberglass tape. The edge can be quite sharp. I have a number of incidents when I released the hold dial on the fiberglass and it sliced my fingers. Practice with your measuring tape and observe safety always.

Yard/Meter Stick

When you have a piece of long fabric that needs to be marked, a meter stick is best to use. Usually, you lay the fabric on a flat surface and proceed to measuring using the meter stick. The rigidity of the stick helps you guide the main frame of the design and allows the cloth to be manipulated. You may even use the meter stick to smoothly drape the fabric on the flat surface. Do not use a meter stick for body measurements because it will miss out on the varying proportions of your clients.

Meter sticks can be made of wood or metal. Be sure to clean it properly and avoid dirt and soil from sticking. Place it somewhere cool so that the stick does not warp or fade. Let the tape measure ensure that the measurements are accurate and that you note what units of measure you are using.

Plastic Ruler

A handy measurement tool, the plastic ruler may suffice if you want to take small measurements within the fabric. They are helpful if you want to make minor adjustments during pattern alteration. It is especially useful if you have the transparent type so that you can also see the fabric as you take measurements. The pliability of the ruler allows for both straight and curve lines of short distances. Do not use this tool if you are taking body measurements or long fabric measurements.

Make sure to store plastic rulers in a cool environment. They are very prone to warping and thus increasing inaccuracy in measurement. Be careful not to let it come in contact with hot iron or chemicals because it may damage the ruler completely.

Seam Gauge

For those venturing into alterations as a profession, you may want to have a seam gauge. This tool is good for measuring short and repeated distances. What is good with the seam gauge is that it allows you to make marks on the fabric because it has a hole to accommodate a pin or a pencil. You may use this if for making patterns or knitting. It can even serve as a compass to make curves and circles pivoting on a center.

Hem Marker

When you are working with skirts, the hemline is important to measure. The hem marker is a measuring tool that rests on a firm base with an adjustable marker that runs vertically. This will let you determine how high you want your hemline to be in relation to the floor. If you are targeting a particular height, there are hem markers that can be pressed to release a powder-like chalk or talcum on the specific measurement. There are other models that have a clamp where you can put the skirt in and mark. You will want a hem marker to make sure that both sides of the skirt are symmetrical when draped properly. Problems arise when you just measure with a tape measure or a yard stick, but upon fitting, one side may lie lower than the other. The goal for skirts is also not to drag on the floor but also to achieve a certain distance from the ground according to the look your client may have.

Essential: Tape measure and yard stick

Nice to have: Plastic ruler, seam gauge and hem marker

Marking Tools

Marking becomes important when you begin transferring the pattern to the fabric. Patterns are your drawing board, the design you want the shirt, trouser or hem to look like. We will discuss more about pattern-making in another chapter, but it is enough that you understand how important they are in clothes construction. Like an engineer with a sketch of the proposed building, your pattern will reflect the final look of your clothes. It then becomes tricky to transfer that plan to an actual fabric. The goal here is to mark the fabric as accurately as the pattern sketch. The markings cannot be too conspicuous or fixed as they will be difficult to remove from the fabric. A good balance of easy transferability and erasable marking is thus targeted.

Dressmaker Tracing Paper

The most inexpensive material for transferring patterns is the tracing paper. The basic steps in marking follow a triple-deck sandwich manner: the pattern or tracing paper placed on a solid surface at the bottom, a thin barrier such as a plastic or tissue paper in between and the fabric on top. Your pattern can be drawn by hand or printed from pre-made sketches. You can use it directly but I recommend you still transfer it first to a tracing paper. Treat the pattern as a master template you can use for other designs. Therefore, to prevent it from being worn out, use a tracing paper instead when transferring to fabric. You can then mark the fabric following the pattern through a number of tools.

You must be able to see the pattern through the fabric. Otherwise, you will need to draw on the fabric. But most patterns are quite transparent allowing for easy transferability. When choosing a tracing paper, make sure that it is a lighter shade than the fabric so it retains the transparency. White is usually preferred as the standard.

When applying the markings on the fabric, be careful with the pressure you use. When you use pointed markers with great or sudden force, this can damage the tracing paper. Some tracing papers can be reused, but the thinness may really compromise the accuracy of the pattern. There are even some materials which can stain the fabric and then through the tracing paper. You have to note how the markings can damage your tracing so that you can avoid these.

Tracing Wheels

The tracing wheel then comes to create the markings on the fabric. This works best for making construction lines for seams or trims.

The way it creates the mark on the fabric is dependent on the model you have. Models are differentiated by the edges with which they make markings. Jagged or saw-toothed types of wheels create the lines by making hard and noticeable lines on the fabric. They can be quite rough on the fabric so be careful because they can damage it easily. Smooth-edged types create less visible markers on the fabric but do not damage the fabric. This is the ideal tracing wheel because it is inexpensive and preserves the integrity of the cloth. Needle-point types are the best and most professional tracing wheel-type available. They provide very subtle markings on the cloth and leave the least amount of damage on the fabric but these models can be quite expensive. It is up to you which model you want to start with; note how these different models can impact your fabric.

Marking Inks

The point of marking inks is for you to make a visible mark on the fabric based on the pattern. It is only used as a guide for you to know where to cut or sew so it must be erasable. You don't want a marking ink to be forever imprinted on the fabric. Hence, erasable marking inks are indispensable in doing alterations. There are a number of such erasable marking inks available on the market. Make sure that they are erasable for all kinds of fabrics. Test them first before you actually buy them.

There are two kinds of these products. The water-based ink creates a mark on the fabric that washes away with water. The ink washes away if you dab it with splotches of water. This ink is more manageable to use and creates even lines on the fabric; make sure that the fabric is not sensitive to water spotting.

The air-based ink can be traced on the fabric if you are a quick worker. This makes a mark on the fabric but disappears spontaneously within a day or two. If you dab it with water, it will disappear instantly. This is good if you are already familiar with the pattern and can do the work within one to two days. If you require more days or there are other alterations to be done on the fabric, the water-based ink may be more appropriate.

Chalk Markers

An alternative to inks are chalk markers. They also mark the fabric well and are easily erasable from the cloth but they can be quite tricky to handle. You would need the pointed chalk markers to outline the fabric well. Chalk markers can come in clay and wax form which are both easy to use. Clay markers also come in two varieties: brick and pencil type. The brick chalk marker comes with a pen-holder while the pencil is already shaped like a pen. Both options mark the fabric equally well. You will, however, need to constantly retrace the lines on the fabric as the brick and pencil markings become weak through repeated use. They are also very fragile so be careful not to drop them. They work in all types of fabric except wool, which will absorb the clay and leave a mark permanently. If you are going to use wool, the wax markers can be more appropriate. The wax marker will leave an oily spot on other fabrics which are not wool. The choice for which marker to use is dependent on the fabric that you will use.

Essential: Dressmaker tracing paper, choice of erasable ink or chalk markers

Nice to have: tracing wheel

Cutting Tools

Once you transfer the pattern into the fabric, you will need to cut the cloth accordingly. You might think that scissors are your only option. Actually, there are a number of cutting tools you can choose from which are more appropriate in certain occasions. Cutting is as crucial as measuring and transferring the pattern into fabric. It is not as simple as hacking away at a piece of cloth. There is an art to a smooth slice. It involves balancing the forces of the cloth being pulled in opposite directions as you cut through it. When cutting, there is a tendency for the cloth to move to a particular side and the measurements can be compromised. Therefore, you need a cutting tool that can slice through the cloth quickly without much resistance as to avoid any deviation from the intended cut.

When you are using a set of cutting tools, make sure that they are only used for that purpose. Do not use a pair of scissors that you are also using for other things such as paper, string, grass, etc. Using the blades on different materials will compromise its sharpness, and through time, will be too blunt to cut through any fabric smoothly. Dedicate your cutting tools only for clothes and store them in a safe place, away from children or near edges.

Most of these cutting tools are made of metal. Make sure that you don't keep them wet or else they will rust fast. Oil them once in a while to keep them working smoothly. Sharpen the edges so that they can cut through smoothly.

Scissors

Of course, you will need a pair of scissors as a basic cutting tool. Surprisingly, scissors are only used when you only need to make small cuts in a fabric. You use scissors to snip at threads when sewing or to correct small uneven lines. They are not used as the primary cutting material for large pieces of cloth. Do not attempt to use scissors with heavy fabrics because you will make the edges blunt while damaging the material unevenly. Like all your cutting tools, you have to keep your scissors sharp. Make sure that the handle fits your fingers well.

Shears

The primary cutting tool for all fabrics are your shears. They are bigger and heavier than your scissors and are therefore more suitable for cutting through large amounts of cloth. They are good with heavy fabric or multiple layers of clothes. You have to be comfortable handling shears well because they can be quite heavy to manipulate. When you feel that the shears are controlling your hand when you cut, then it is not a good fit. You should be in more control, so buy a pair of shears which you can best manipulate or will not cause excessive strain to your hands.

There are many kinds of shears depending on the shape of the edges. There are straight shears which are good for cutting through different types of fabrics at a smooth and fast pace. There are bent shears which are more curved and are appropriate if you really want to aim for accuracy in cutting. Then there are serrated or saw-toothed shears which are more appropriate for fabrics which easily move in place. The serrated edges keep the cloth in place and allows for a straighter cut. Again, choose the type of shears that will match the fabric you are going to work with.

Seam Ripper

You can use scissors if you want to cut through seams which you want to undo but a seam ripper will do the job faster and more efficiently. They can slice between threads and prevent you from damaging the fabric itself. The technique to unzipping stitches without cutting the fabric is to stretch the edges and cut through the stitches one at a time. Do not plod blindly and rip the stitches apart. This creates an uneven cut which will not look good. When one stitch is undone, simply pull the edges more and cut through with the seam ripper.

Essential: Scissors and Shears

Nice to have: Seam Ripper

Sewing Tools

Basic sewing tools are part of the essentials of any tailor. Whether you are more comfortable with hand-sewing or using a machine, you must be very confident in your sewing skills in order to make a good alteration. We will not be teaching sewing techniques in this book because that topic is better discussed in detail in another book. Basic sewing techniques can be learned easily. What you need to start out with are your basic thread and needles. These tools come in different sizes and colors which all depend on the fabric and the pattern you are using.

Thread

Threads come in many colors, materials, and weights and appropriate use must be observed. For example, the choice of the weight of the thread is equivalent to the weight of the fabric it is going to be used for. Delicate fabrics such as sheer and silk will need a light-weight thread. If you use heavier ones, the thread will stand out instead of blending with the fabric. For ordinary fabric, the medium-weight thread will suffice. For heavier cloth, use only the heavy-weight threads to hold the material together.

In terms of color, determine where the stitches will be placed. If you are going to sew a pocket, you can use any color for the inside pockets but if your stitch is somewhere noticeable, use the best approximation for the fabric you are using. Thread colors which clash with the fabric will stand out and that will not look good. The illusion you want to achieve is that the clothes are seamless.

In terms of material, there are a number of threads you can choose from. There are synthetic, cotton, silk and nylon among others. The general principle is of course to choose the material of the thread that closely resembles the fabric material. In general, cotton threads work with almost all fabrics so this will be a good investment.

Hand-sewing Needles

As with thread, needles come in different sizes. It is crucial for you to know basic hand sewing because a machine may bog them at times. So knowing what kind of hand-sewing needle is needed when you are beginning. There are stores which sell needles as a set already, lined according to sizes. The smallest are called your 'betweens' which you will use most of the time; because they are small, they allow for more accurate sewing. These needles may be difficult to manipulate if you have large fingers. The next size is called 'sharps.' They are longer and can be used if you are sewing through different layers or across greater distances. They are less accurate but they can accommodate more fabric. The biggest needles are called 'milliners' which also have large eyes. They are only good for basting long seams. Know which size is appropriate for the type of sewing you will be doing.

The thinness and thickness of needles also vary. The general principle is use thinner ones for lighter fabric and use thicker ones for heavy fabric. The goal of the needles is just to pierce through the fabric and hold the thread together. You must find that good balance so that your sewing can be uninterrupted.

Machine-sewing Needles

If you are really into alteration or making clothes in general, investing in a sewing machine can be a game-changer. It speeds up the work and allows you to manipulate fabrics in a more efficient way. There are several sewing machines in the market and you have to find one which you feel comfortable with. Choose a machine that is affordable and durable, that is perfect for your sitting height and will not cause undue strain, and that fits your working space well.

As with hand-sewing needles, machine needles also vary in sizes according to the fabric you are going to use. The principle also holds true that you use smaller or thinner needles for more delicate fabrics and for accurate stitching. Use thicker or longer needles for heavier or multiple fabrics.

Some tips on using the machine. Do not stitch over pins. I know this might be self-evident, but it happens a lot of times, especially when tailors forget to remove them. When the needle head hits the pin, the needle itself can be broken or chipped. If you do it repeatedly, the needle can be too blunt to sew properly so make sure that you remove the pins before stitching with the machine.

Pins and pin cushions

Another essential tool for any tailor are your pins. When you want to fit the clothes on a client, you use a pin to hold the fabric together at certain points. You can use pins to mark areas for measurement or cutting and to hold the fabric in place. Just be careful that you don't stick the client when you are applying the pin on the clothes. It is not a good experience to be pricked by a pin accidentally.

Pins also come in varying sizes and thickness according to your need. Follow the size principle of shorter pins for thinner fabric, longer pins for thicker or multiple fabrics. The type of pin will be more important. Pins like those made from brass or nickel do not rust easily, while stainless ones can corrode occasionally. Do not use rusted ones anymore because they may be a source of infection.

For safety, always place your active pins in a pin cushion. Do not leave your pins lying all around. They have plastic heads which easily roll and can disappear in the carpet until somebody unfortunate enough steps on them. Place the pins on the cushion all the time when you are not using them.

Thimble

Not many people know how to use a thimble. As a tailor, it is one of your best tools to prevent sewing injury. Usually, accidents occur when you are stitching very fast and the needle pricks your middle finger. To prevent this, you place a thimble on this finger so you can avoid a painful accident and also prevent staining the fabric with blood. You want to make a good impression on your client so practice safety always.

Essentials: thread, hand-sewing needles, pins and pin cushions, thimble

Nice to have: sewing machine and needles

Accessories

Though not directly part of the sewing process, the measuring and fitting experience of your clients will need a few supplies. When a customer comes to you, your materials for measuring and fitting the clothes on them must be complete. Otherwise, you end up losing time as you look for tools when you need them at the moment. Have a kit on hand with you whenever you are entertaining a client. This assures you that you have everything on hand as the need arises.

Mirror

A full-body mirror is essential in any alteration shop or even at home. You need your client to be able to see his/herself fully. They need to see their anatomical body, their shape and contour, the proportions and the parts they want to highlight or hide. You also want them to see their back and their sides which they don't usually see. Some are very conscious of their figure so it is good to have them see themselves from all sides. Of course, you want them to see how the clothes look on them from all angles. You are selling your creation to them and the mirror is the best convincing agent you can use. When clients see for themselves that the clothes look good on them, they will return to you. If you hand over the altered clothes in a bag, there is not much connection between the two of you and there is a chance the client will need you to redo the alteration. Make the mirror your ally by allowing clients to see how good they look in your creation.

Notepad/Notebook

Take note of all measurements of your clients in one notebook. This is going to be your Bible of measurements so keep this very safe. When you have a notebook on hand, you don't forget the measurements at all. It is very frustrating for customers to be fitted with a tape measure over and over again because the tailor forgot the measurement. It is more disappointing to mess up your measurements because you forgot some crucial ones. You may have excellent memory but a notebook is more sharp than you are.

Plus, when you record measurements, you have a history of your clients. You will be able to record their growth over the years. You can say that they were size 28 ten years ago or a medium when they were younger. This helps you build rapport with them because you are able to remember all these tiny details about them. Loyalty is developed when customers feel that you really know them.

Corrugated Cardboard

When working with fabric, always have a flat surface. You want a steady base because your materials may slip and fall in all sorts of directions. Create a workstation in your room where you can place your materials safely. The cardboard can even have measurements on it for quick reference. You can use the board as a base to sketch patterns, drape fabrics, temporarily place pins, etc. The board also protects your table from damage. It is worth investing on a good corrugated cardboard because you will be using that on the table a lot.

These are the range of tools you will need when beginning to fit and alter clothes. I can never overemphasize the need to take care of your tools because they can last for a lifetime. Practice safety always so don't leave sharp objects just lying around. You don't need to buy expensive equipment if you are just starting out. Please do buy quality and durable materials because that can really affect the accuracy of your measurements and stitches. As a summary, I would like to recommend a list of essentials needed for your journey towards becoming a great alterations tailor:

1. Tape measure

2. Yard stick

3. Tracing paper

4. Erasable ink or chalk markers

5. Scissors

6. Shears

7. Thread

8. Hand-sewing needles

9. Thimble

10. Pins and pin cushions

11. Notepad

12. Corrugated cardboard

Chapter Summary

In this chapter, I have learned that:

- Alteration tools belong to five categories: measuring, marking, cutting, sewing, and accessories.

- It is worthwhile to invest on good quality materials.

- It is important to maintain the sewing materials in good condition as they affect the accuracy of measurements.

In the next chapter you will learn how to select patterns.

Chapter Two:
Selecting Patterns

Any alteration starts with a pattern. A pattern is simply a template of a dress, a skirt, a shirt or any piece of clothing that is transferred to the fabric to make clothes. There are many commercially-produced patterns available for males and females, for children and for adults. In determining the pattern to be used, there are two important questions you need to ask:

1. What is the body size and measurement of your client?

2. What are the patterns suitable for your client?

We will discuss these two crucial questions in this chapter. It is important for you to know that there must be a great harmony between your client's body measurements and the pattern you are going to choose. When your pattern does not fit your client, whether it is too small, too large, too tight or too loose, then your client becomes frustrated. You have to practice the art of matching the body size to the pattern. This will entail meeting a lot of clients and becoming familiar with a lot of available patterns.

First, you must have a good gauge of your client's body. Manufacturers will usually design patterns for an ideal figure from a statistical mean of all bodies studied. Remember, each client will be different. When you evaluate your client's body, do not look at them as they should look like. Observe them for what they really are, and most of the time this deviates from the standard. You can accomplish this observation through the following methods:

- Mirror technique: Have the client face the mirror from the front, both sides and the back. Take time for each angle and notice every part of the body. It may be good to divide the body into 'heads.' Imagine that you are taking the size of the client's head and divide down, from the neck to the bust, to the waist, to the hips, etc. Note the natural posture of the client. While it is good for the client to always stand upright and tall, they usually don't in real life. The clothes may fit them well when they are standing tall, but will look loose or tight when they slouch in real life. Note all these changes and record them in your notebook.

- Photograph: Take pictures of the client from the front, both sides and the back. Ask for permission if you can store their picture for reference purposes. What is good with this technique is that you have at-hand access to the client's figure. In the mirror technique, you will have to rely on your memory of that measurement event and the objective tape measures. With a photograph, you can always refer back to the client whenever you want to confirm anything. Be careful that these photos remain private. Delete them as soon as the alteration is finished. Some clients will not agree to this because it may seem too intrusive, but explain to them the benefits of this method.

- Use a tape measure: The fool-proof method is really to take the client's measurements. We will discuss later on all the measurements you will need to take. This step is indispensable in every alteration project. This will serve as your objective guide in choosing the pattern and altering the clothes to fit your client. I highly suggest that you write all the measurements with the date taken and the units properly labeled. This will be your reference point for the client's measurements. They are specific to the date so you have to repeat the measurement at every point they come to you. Do not assume that they have the same measurements from last year or from ten years back. Measure them every time they come for an alteration.

I would recommend that you do all three techniques for every client visit. Some will object to having their photograph taken. At the very least, you must accomplish the mirror and tape measurement techniques.

Next, body sizes are different from males and females, children and adults. The same person will not have the same measurement as they age. It is good to know the standards for each age group and gender. Know that every client will differ from the standard, however minimally. The recommended sizes I will tell you will not always apply to your clients. Hence, customize it to how they really measure up, not just what their measurements should be.

There are three important measurements that will determine the pattern you are going to use: the height and build, the circumference, and the posture of the client. Each of these measurements provide a unique factor in determining which pattern to use. The height and build of the client will determine the pattern figure type. The circumference will determine the number size. Finally, the posture of the client will determine the pattern company you should be choosing from.

Height and Build

I will be discussing now the different standards of measurements for each gender and the age groups. When I say that the ideal height for a 36 year old male is 5 feet 10 inches, you know that this does not apply to everyone. I indicate the ideal to give you an idea of how pattern companies make their templates. In the end, the actual measurement of the client determines the pattern type you will use. You can have a 36 year old male whose height and build are more of a teen boy's type. You don't follow the age of the client; you follow their actual measurements.

When you measure the height and build, it may be good to measure the back as the reference. Start measuring from the most prominent upper vertebra, around the area they call as C7 or cervical bone 7. You can feel this as the spine bone that is most pointed and palpable at the level of the neck area, opposite the throat. Measure from this level to the level of the waist to get the height. For purposes of standardization, I will be using feet and inches to describe these measurements. Make sure that you are using the same measuring system or that you know the conversion to your preferred measuring system. You can go back to Chapter One to refer to the measuring tools for the conversion factors.

For Children

There are really no pattern distinctions between male and female children. The differences between the body types of the sexes are more apparent when puberty hits. Hence, this age group has one pattern for both sexes. They are all divided into toddlers and children.

Toddlers have a height of 28 to 40 inches. These are usually babies or those just beginning to walk. The shirt or dress is shorter than the entire length of the child. In terms of pants, the hips are larger and the crotch sizes are bigger to accommodate for a diaper.

Children pattern types are for those 35 to 48 inches long. The body length is of course bigger than the toddler size and the crotch depth is shorter because children will not usually require a diaper.

For Males

Body types are categorized according to boys, teens and men. The maximum pattern size is fitted for a height of 5 feet 10 inches. Individuals taller than that would still use the pattern for men with major alterations.

Boys' size types are good for those ranging from 48 to 58 inches. A basic bodice sloper is used for this age group. We will discuss slopers later on, but this basically means a dress template resembling the body. From the children's, the boy's size type has a wider shoulder for the shirt and a longer trouser length.

Teen Boys' size types are for those ranging from 5 feet 1 inch to 5 feet 8 inches tall. They are wider in shoulder length and longer in trouser length as compared to boys' sizes.

Men's size types are designed for those reaching 5 feet 10 inches. You will need to alter the pattern if your client is shorter or taller in height or bigger or smaller than the average size. You can make alterations for length and width from above and below the waist. The shoulders are quite similar to teen sizes.

For Females

Females have a wider range of sizes to accommodate the many bodily changes they have. For the height and build, we will not be incorporating the bust size yet, though it will affect these. The circumference measurements are most appropriate for the bust.

There are seven sizes for females according to body height and length. These are:

1. Girls's size type for those 50 to 61 inches tall.

2. Young Junior or Teen for those 5 feet 1 inch to 5 feet 3 inches tall.

3. Junior petite for those 5 feet 4 inches to 5 feet 5 inches tall.

The next sizes are for those with a more developed, mature body type. The height may overlap with the previous set, but the difference is in the body maturity.

1. Half size for those 5 feet 2 inches to 5 feet 3 inches.

2. Miss petite for those 5 feet 2 inches to 5 feet 4 inches.

3. Misses for those 5 feet 5 inches to 5 feet 6 inches.

4. Women: 5 feet 5 inches to 5 feet 6 inches.

For the half size, these are more for women who have narrower shoulders and short back waist length. The hips and the waist are also larger compared to the other types. We use the women's size type for those who have the height of the Misses, but have increased circumferences or build.

Circumference

There are two important measurements to determine the circumference of the person: the bust and the hips. Remember that these measurements are very particular in terms of age and gender. Bust and hip sizes change through the differently bodily developments as people change.

Bust

When you want to make dresses, blouses, coats, jackets or vests, the bust size is important. You measure it at the level of the elbow, rounding at the upper portion of each breast to consider the greatest circumference. Breasts may differ in size on the left and the right so just take the biggest measurement of the two. For women, you have to take the over bust, the bust and the under bust size, while for men, only one notation is used.

If the client has a cup A bra or a large bone structure, you can use a larger pattern size than recommended. Remember that it is easier to adjust the width or circumference of the clothes than the proportion at the shoulders and the arms. Having a larger size will accommodate the other body proportions and you can simply alter the width to make it smaller.

If the client has a bra cup size C or has a smaller bone structure, use a smaller pattern size than the recommended. This will fit better into the overall proportion of the person considering the shoulders and the arm length. You can simply adjust the width of the pattern.

Hips

When you want to make pants and skirts, the hips are important to measure. Look for the bony prominence on the side of the body below the belly button and that is the most likely location of the hips. From the hip measurement, you can adjust the pattern according to the size of the buttocks, the thighs, and the crotches. These are easily altered, but you have to get the hip measurement right.

Posture

The way a person is built and carries his or herself will determine which pattern company you will use. There are five established companies and they cater to a particular frame. When estimating the build of a person, have them stand tall first so you can assess the full height. Turn them to the side so you can see the width. Then, have them stand as they naturally do, without exerting effort. That effortless stance is the person's posture. Pattern companies specialize on particular frames in making their patterns.

McCall is a pattern company that specializes on average to tall figures, with a more prominent upper back than others. The bodice is longer and wider than all the other pattern companies. The bust tip is positioned ¼ to ½ inch higher and 5/6 inches farther from the center. This indicates a bustier figure.

In terms of sleeve caps, it is shorter and narrower than other patterns. Elbow circumference is also larger and the dart is transferred to the wrist level. This allows for a wider forearm circumference.

The skirt also has the widest width and the longest hem of all the patterns. The front waist dart is placed near the hip bones around a third the distance from the side to the center front. There is also more sloping from the hem to the waistline.

Butterick and Vogue cater to the average to tall figures. We take them as one category because their pattern sizes do not differ very much.

The bodice is shorter than McCall's by ¼ inch on the back. The shoulder and the width across the shoulder blades are the narrowest of the patterns.

The front neck width is curved less than McCall. The bust tip is placed lower than all of the patterns. The center length in the waist area is longer than McCall's by 1/6 inches. The sleeve cap is placed higher and is wider than all of the patterns. The sleeve fits tighter than most to allow the elbow more room to move.

The skirt hips are smaller compared to McCall's. The side seam is not sloping and is almost straight. There are two darts for the front and another two darts at the back skirt which is unique to these two companies. The front darts divide the hips and waist in thirds. The back dart accommodates the upper hip and the buttock areas.

Simplicity designs for the average to shorter individuals. The back bodice length is shorter than Butterick and Vogue by 1/8 inches. The arm joints are slightly forwarded based on the back shoulder slope. The chest width is the narrowest of the patterns. The bust tip is at the same height as McCall. It has the same center length in the waist area like Butterick and Vogue.

The sleeve caps are shorter than Butterick and Vogue by ¼ inches, with the same elbow width as McCall. The basic dart is moved towards the wrist level to allow more width for the forearm.

Individuals with a smaller frame are more appropriate for Burda patterns. The upper back is slightly rounded and the arm joints are forwarded as evidenced by the dart size and the shoulder slope. The back bodice is shorter than Simplicity by 1/8 inches. The width of the lower bodice is narrower than the American sizes. there is a shorter side seam and a bigger underarm dart. The bust tip is at the same level as Butterick and Vogue.

The sleeve circumference is the smallest of all the patterns. The elbow dart is also placed higher. The sleeve cap is designed for thin arms.

In terms of skirts, it is wider than Butterick and Vogue but not as wide as McCall. The side seam is slightly more sloped than Butterick and Vogue. The basic dart is placed near the hemline to allow more room for thigh and hip movement. The front and back width is the same as Simplicity.

Taken together, you must take note of the person's height and built, circumference and posture. All of these will determine the pattern you will use. Take the actual measurement of the client when you saw him or her, and not the measurements from before. The body undergoes many changes so the most reliable are the most recent measurements.

When you begin working with patterns, you will encounter two kinds: the sloper and the block patterns. The sloper pattern is more appropriate for your level. A sloper is often called the 'second skin' because it closely resembles the human body measurement. It is a pattern that is made from draping muslins on a model or dressform following body measurements. Since it uses the exact measurements, it does not allow for any movement if worn. It represents the most basic form of pattern which most home-sewers use. You will alter the sloper then according to the measurements of your client and the design you will incorporate.

You will be working with six kinds of slopers: the front and back bodice, the front and back skirt, the sleeves and the pants. From this base, slopers will come out the different dress forms if you now want to expand the outline. For example, the front and back bodices can be turned into your shirts, jackets, coats and blouses.

A block is a combination of slopers to produce the final pattern so you can combine a bodice and pant sloper to make a jumpsuit or a bodice and skirt to make a dress pattern. These are usually made by manufacturers. Blocks allow for different movements by creating seam and wearing ease allowances. They expand the sloper form into something more wearable. For your level, you can start with the slopers first and then try to combine them to form different blocks. The pattern construction is designed for particular people. You can edit pre-made slopers or you can even design and create customized slopers on your own.

For males, you can construct slopers into shirts, hood jackets, trousers and denim pants. You can create blocks from blazers by combining bodice and sleeve slopers. For females, you can create slopers into blouses, jackets and skirts. You can combine slopers into blocks by pairing bodice with skirts to make a party dress or a tunic. The basic dress forms can be expanded if you use different fabrics, different sizes and lengths, different accessories and pleatings. All of these will start with slopers and blocks.

Chapter Summary

In this chapter, I have learned that:

- To select a pattern, you must know the client's height and build, circumference and posture.

- Height and built are particular for different age groups and for men and women.

- There are five basic company patterns based on posture: McCall, Butterick and Vogue, Simplicity and Burda.

In the next chapter you will learn what fitting standards are.

Chapter Three:
Fitting Standards

Have you ever seen ill-fitting clothes? What was your reaction? Of course, as an alterations tailor, people would come to us because they feel that their clothes don't fit them. We are so used to learning what should look good, we are trained to see what others don't. For example, if the skirt is too short or too tight, the person wearing it may feel restricted in terms of movement. It may draw unwanted attention and cause a scandal to conservatives. Or a baggy pair of trousers will always droop no matter how often you pull them up. A loose shirt may not always look fashionable and give the appearance of sloppiness. There is always a sense of wrongness visually when you see ill-fitting clothes on a person.

Of course, not everyone is gifted to be anatomically symmetrical. We may see models showing off their perfectly symmetric bodies in various fashion shows. They are more of the exception than the rule. All of us have some sort of imbalance, however minimal. As we age, even the most symmetrical body may develop some skewness. Some are leaning more towards the left, others are too busty or flat, hips may be drooping to one side. The clothes then follow these asymmetries and if not corrected, can highlight such differences. Since clothes are based on perfectly symmetrical bodies, they will not always look good as they are bought on ordinary people. If a skirt is drooping on one side, the other will compensate by lifting higher. With these variations in proportion, achieving harmony and balance becomes a challenge. When we know proper fitting principles, then clothes can transform asymmetric bodies into well-balanced forms.

Therefore, how clothes fit is important in any fashion designer or tailor. We want to create clothes that look good and fit well on people. This is achieved when we see a sense of harmony in the clothes. This means that all elements to the clothes contribute to the overall aesthetic beauty of the final look. One component of harmony is balance. We expect that when you wear anything, the right is balanced with the left, the front is balanced with the back. When we see a skirt from afar, we want to see that the right part of the skirt is hanging at the same level as the left. Otherwise, we say that the clothes don't fit the person. The balance is off and the harmony is disrupted, producing an overall bad look on the person.

Balance is achieved by two methods: the grainline and the structural line. These two contribute to the overall sense of balance in the clothes and how the clothes look on the person. The grainline focuses on the fabric, while the structural line integrates the clothes to the anatomic body.

First, the grainline refers to the alignment of elements in a fabric. Think of grainlines as imaginary horizontal and vertical lines lying perpendicular to each other in a fabric. This is easy to imagine in a fabric which is quilted or woven. We say that the garment has symmetric grainlines when elements of the clothes lie within these imaginary perpendicular lines. This can be challenging to imagine in fabrics that don't have explicit lines such as floral patterns or textured fabrics.

The grainline also is not just confined to the fabric itself, but also to the arrangement of fabric as a garment or a finished clothes. The designer can position the garment to be aligned to the grainline by manipulating the fabric so that its elements lie perpendicular to each other and the body. To help you remember the grainlines on a garment, mark vertical lines on the center front and back, the mid-front and mid-back, the sleeve capline and the seams on the side. They must all be parallel to each other. To mark the horizontal lines, place imaginary lines on the shoulder blade, the chest, the bust, the waist, the hips and the sleeve capline. All of these must be parallel to each other and to the ground. You have to train yourself in looking for the grainline in clothes to see if all the elements are aligned. If you still find it difficult to see the grainline just by looking, you can attach a weight on a string and place it on either side of the garment. The balance is achieved when both strings are hanging parallel to each other. From, here, you can appreciate the grainline.

Next, you can also achieve balance by observing the structural lines. This refers to how the elements in the clothes align with the anatomic body. We want to see clothes that mimic the symmetry (or the corrected symmetry) of a body. So like the grainline, we use the body references for vertical and horizontal lines (the center front and back and the hips for example). Next, we compare the different elements in clothes that should correspond as parallel to those imaginary perpendicular lines. We expect that the seams, darts, tucks, pleats and other elements of the clothes lie parallel either to the horizontal or vertical lines of the body. Otherwise, the garment will stick out or the body will look imbalanced.

When you construct clothes, you also have to consider the ease of the clothes. This refers to the lack of tension on the appearance of the clothes. There are two kinds: the wearing and design ease. The wearing ease refers to the degree of comfort the person wearing the clothes experience when moving with it. You want clothes where the person can be free to move forwards, backward, side to side without becoming stiff. Beautiful clothes which restrict movement may not be very sellable. We want to make the clothes as relaxing for the wearer that is why we have to create wearing ease on the clothes. This may mean allowing for extra fabrics on slopers. The second kind of ease refers to design. The designer can put various elements on a basic sloper such as pleats or pockets. These designs do not affect the movement of the person, but can contribute to the overall aesthetic merit of the garment. All of these elements must still conform to the overall balance of the clothes.

There are many elements that can be used to achieve this design ease. This includes: pockets, collars, darts, drapes, gathers, pleats and slits, and flares. We will discuss how each must be placed to achieve balance.

Pockets

Pockets can both be functional or decorative or a combination of both. They can be conspicuous or hidden. They can lie in the outward garment surface, inserted inside as a slash, or hidden in a seam. When you design pockets, they should be proportional to the overall garment and placed within the grainline and structural lines. When the pocket is placed in a body curve such as the hips, they should lie flat and smooth, not jutting out. The garment must also be designed to be loose enough so that the inside pockets do not become visible or that outer pocket openings remain closed.

Collars

Collars allow for a sense of depth in a garment. They hang around the neck and can be used to conceal scarfs or neckties. They are classified as flat, standing band, full roll or partial roll. The collar must be comfortable around the neck of the person, not causing undue strain. The outer edge of the collar must cover the back of the neckline and be placed smoothly on the garment. The ends should lie symmetrically. Lapels should be proportionate to the body. If you are going to change the garment neckline or the slope of the shoulders, the collar will also need to be changed accordingly. When one shoulder is slouching on one side, you can achieve balance by making the collar on the affected side smaller or shorter than the other.

Darts

You will see darts as the lines fabrics make when they are fitted on people, like fabric creases. Darts must give a feeling of lightness and symmetry. If you have one dart, it will enhance a body bulge. If you have two or more darts, they are placed parallel to the central bulge. This de-emphasizes areas where you don't want other people to see a bulge such as the stomach. Therefore, bigger body types will need more darts to create the illusion of smallness.

Gathers

Gathers are loose collections of fabric that hang on the edges of clothes to achieve a sense of lightness or fullness. Examples of gathers include bishop or puffed sleeves, a harem skirt or a blouson bodice. These tiny folds emanating from a single point gives an illusion of volume. For gathers that are controlled from the top, the edges should fall vertically parallel to the body line. For gathers that are controlled from the top and the bottom, there should be enough length as not to restrict movement.

Pleats

Pleats are usually long lines that extend from the top to the bottom of a garment created to add style to the garment such as umbrella or accordion pleats. The pleats must be controlled in such a way that they retain their shape even when the person is moving. When a pleat is placed on a bulge, you will need to create a lining. The garment must be tension-less even with such bold lines marking the garment.

Flares

A flare can be placed on the free edge of garments that creates the illusion of fullness or lightness. You can place flares in areas which are within the grainline especially on skirts and blouses. Because they divide the body into panels, flares must be symmetric and evenly-spaced. The flares you placed on one side must balance with the flares on the other side.

Chapter Summary

In this chapter, I have learned that:

- Clothes are assessed by how they follow the grainline and structure lines as the standard fitting patterns.

- There are garment fitting elements like pleats, gathers, tucks, vents, slits, darts, collars, drapes and pockets.

In the next chapter you will learn methods of pattern fitting.

Chapter Four:
Methods of Pattern Fitting

You picked out a pattern based on the client's height and built, circumference and posture. The next step is to fit the pattern to the specification of the person. Do not wait until you finish the garment before fitting it to the client. The most efficient way of proceeding with alteration is to customize the pattern first to the client before executing it on fabric. Make sure that you find a time to meet with your client to fit the pattern.

When you are fitting a client with patterns, utilize your full length mirror to analyze your client. Let them stand in a comfortable position, advising them to assume a good posture so that the final fit would be perfect. Provide a space where they can privately change. too cramped quarters may force them to assume positions they are not comfortable with. Advise them to wear snug-fitting underwear that they can comfortably display. Fitting involves some degree of intimacy with your client so make sure that they also feel comfortable to be in their underwear with your presence.

There are three methods of fitting patterns on your clients: pinned, trial garment and measurement methods. Choose the one that you feel most comfortable with. They are arranged here in the order most appropriate for beginners to experts. When starting out, it is good to use the pinned pattern. As you fit more clients, you will have a greater pattern and fitting sense so you can proceed with the other pattern fitting methods. Just make sure that you don't cause too much stress on your client with the fitting method you use.

Pinned Method

This pattern fitting method uses cutouts of your pattern and you literally fit them on the client. What is good with this method is that you don't use up the fabric itself before you actually need to cut it. This is the quickest fitting method to use so you don't delay the project. Since you are working just with paper patterns, you will need to exert more effort at imagining how the actual fabric will look like. But this method is best for figures who are easy to fit or if you are making loose garments.

As we have explained, slopers are the basic patterns you will encounter. When you are assembling the slopers into blocks or into a complete dress, it is good that you have a sense of how to place them. Do not make them too far apart from each other as when assembling the sleeves with the bodice. It will make the client bigger than they actually are. Do not place the patterns too close together because it will then give a false illusion of being too small. The proper method is really to overlap the patterns with allowances for movement. The overlap must just be right that will make the wearer comfortable when just standing and also moving about.

Before Fitting

I will now outline some basic steps on how to assemble the pattern before you meet a client. Do not assemble the patterns only when the client is there because it does take up a lot of time. I will also emphasize ways on how to strengthen your paper patterns so they do not become damaged during the fitting procedure.

1. Cut the individual pattern pieces with allowances. Do not cut too close to the edges since you still want to have the choice of adjusting the final pattern piece.

2. Reinforce your paper patterns. You can use either a cardboard, a sewing cutting board or a corkboard. This will prevent your pattern from becoming damaged from use. Simply place the pattern on the cardboard and cut around the edges. To make them stick to each other, you can use an aluminum foil in between the board and the paper pattern. Iron the three pieces so they adhere. You can even add a plastic wrap to cover all the pattern units.

3. When working with the crotch, neckline, arms and waistline, trim the excess patterns.

4. When placing the darts, make sure that the pin goes through and through the pattern to secure it.

5. Align the seam allowances by overlapping them along the stitching lines. To avoid any injury, make sure that the pins are placed horizontally or parallel to the stitching lines. Be careful about handling the patterns, remembering where the pins are placed.

6. Assemble all the pattern pieces together to remember how the garment will look like. It is important that you know how the patterns are related so that you can focus on the fit on the client. It is embarrassing to meet a client and you are still struggling where parts go together.

During Fitting

1. Prepare the client beforehand. Prompt them that you will be assembling the pieces on them to see the actual fit.

2. Start from the least complex to the most complex pattern pieces. Start with the skirt, then the vest, the bodice or the jacket and end with the sleeves.

3. To secure the pattern on the person, place a fitting band around the armpits or the armscye, the waist and the hips.

    a. To do this, first, place the fitting band underneath or around the body part (armscye, waist or hips) and then secure with a pin.

    b. Make two markings on the band. First on the endfold and the other on the exact spot where the fold is located. This is the center front.

    c. Remove the band and fold them in between the two markings. Again, mark the midpoint this time as 'center back.'

    d. Ensure that the markings are aligned. Use the bands to make sure that the pattern pieces don't fall off.

4. For skirts and trousers

    a. Lift the skirt pattern piece to the waist line and the hips, making sure that the center front and back are aligned. Place the stitching line of the waist at the bottom of the band.

5. For the bodice

    a. Place the bodice pattern in your model. Make sure that the arms go through the armscye first and then bring the pattern piece down the person. to test for movement, let the person place her hands on the hips or on the back of her head

6. Sleeves

    a. With the bodice piece already in place, slide the sleeve piece into the arms and fasten with the bands. Overlap the sleeve caps on the bodice and make sure that the arm can move freely. `

7. Make the necessary adjustment on the pattern pieces. If there are areas where you feel should be extended or cut, place markings on the target areas. If you want to remove areas on the pattern piece, you can simply fold it over so that you reach the desired length. If you want to increase the size of the pattern piece, you can insert extra pattern paper and fasten it with pins. Evaluate if all the hemlines are symmetrically in place. This is the part where you have to make all the necessary adjustments.

8. Make sure that everything is aligned. All vertical centers should align with the body centers. Dart lines should point to the fullest body bulge. Make sure that the client is comfortable with the pattern pieces in place both at rest and during movement.

9. Remove the pattern pieces and make sure that all the markings are intact. It is better to make the adjustments out of the model when the alterations are quite numerous.

10. Make the necessary changes on the pattern pieces.
    Utilize the pivot, seam or slash methods for areas
    where you pin or tuck-marked.

After Fitting

1. Make sure that all the markings are intact. Store them
   in a safe place until you will be transferring the
   pattern to fabric.

2. If the pattern has major revisions, it may be more
   useful to make a new pattern piece incorporating all
   the edits. Do not rely on the extra paper you pinned
   on the pieces while you were fitting if you want to
   increase the size. It is really better to have one solid
   piece of perfectly-matched pattern pieces rather than
   separate pieces.

Trial Garment Method

This method is ideal for those with atypical figures or
variations from the standard. It may be too tedious or time-
consuming for some, but how it fits the person will be more
accurate in this method rather than the pinning method.
This method is basically making an actual garment using an
inexpensive fabric and trying it on the model. Usually, a
muslin is used as the trial fabric to cut expenses and to
manipulate the fabric quickly. If the texture is going to be a
major issue, try to get the closest possible fabric with the
same texture as the real one. When basting, you can choose
to hand-sew or use a machine for quick sewing. Make sure
that the trial garment is well-made and will not rip when
fitted. This method will involve four stages: pattern
preparation, fabric preparation, assembling the garment and
fitting the garment.

Pattern Preparation

1. Cut all the pattern pieces you will need. Give generous allowances because you will still need to adjust. It is better to have more allowance than cutting the pattern too close to the actual.

2. On each pattern piece, indicate the lengthwise fitting at the center of the pattern.

   a. On the pants, half lengthwise at the level of the knee and extend through the whole pattern.

   b. On the bodices, indicate the center back and center front.

   c. On the sleeve, fold lengthwise at the level above the elbow and extend.

3. On each pattern piece, indicate the crosswise fitting at the center of the pattern. Mark the lines along the sleeve capline, chest, shoulder blades, and hips as they are all parallel to the hemline at the ground.

Fabric Preparation

1. Assess the grainline of the fabric. Make sure that the lines of the fabric are lying perpendicular to each other.

2. Place the pattern pieces corresponding to the grainline of the fabric. Mark pins to keep the pieces in place. Reinforce the pattern along the pattern pieces with more pins.

3. Add more pins around 2 inches away from the pattern pieces in the fabric itself. The fabric will move when

you begin to cut it so it is good to have reinforcements
both inside and beyond the pattern pieces.

4. Begin cutting the fabric along the pattern pieces.
   Make allowances for alteration.

5. Transfer the center front and back, the crosswise and
   lengthwise markings from the pattern to the fabric
   using a pencil. These will be important for assembly.

Constructing the garment

1. Place the pieces on a flat surface. Overlap them at the
   stitching lines to see the complete garment assembled.

2. You can baste the patterns through a number of ways.

   a. Pin-basting: From one end, fold the fabric along a
      dartline. Lay the fold symmetrically on the other
      and secure with a pin. Make the seam lines of the
      separate pieces meet and secure with a pin.

   b. Hand-basting: Do the pin-basting first as noted
      above. Then, do slip-basting along the folded
      edges.

   c. Machine-basting: Make sure that you are stitching
      the seam allowances and the darts inside the
      garment. Start with the longest stitch and sew
      without creating tension on the garment.

Fitting the garment

1. Start fitting the pieces separately starting from the
   easiest to the most complex. Start with the skirt, then
   the bodice, then the sleeves last.

2. Make the necessary adjustment on the garment as it is fitted on the model. If it is too tight, loosen some of the stitches and re-stitch. If the garment is too loose, pin tuck the garment and then stitch until the desired length is achieved.

3. Ensure that fitting standards are in place.

4. If all the adjustments have been made, stitch the trial garment as a single garment. Be aware of the hem as it should be symmetrical. Try it on the model again and create the final adjustments.

Measurement Method

This method is the most convenient for clients because they do not have to change clothes or have patterns or garments attached to them. All you need to do in this method is to take their bodily measurements. This is quite tricky because you have to complete all measurements on the client because you don't have the benefit of a trial garment or a pinned pattern. You will be transferring the measurements on actual fabric so the leeway for error is smaller compared to the other methods. I recommend this method if you have been measuring a lot of people and that you are confident that you are accurate in your measurements. We will be discussing all the measurements on the different body segments for each pattern piece.

Lower Body (for making skirts and trousers)

1. Centers: measure from the waist at the bellybutton level to the floor.

2. Inseam: measure from the crotch to the floor.

3. Knee position: measure from the middle of the kneecap to the floor.

4. Side seam: measure from above the hips to the floor.

5. Hip depth: measure from the waist to the hip joint at the center front, back, and both sides.

6. Crotch length: measure from the center waistline front to the center waistline back passing through the crotch.

7. Waist circumference: measure from center back to the both sides. Measure center front waist to both sides. Record the two measurements.

8. Hip circumference: measure from center back hips to both sides. Measure center hip front to both sides. Record the two measurements. Take into account the size of the buttocks.

9. Thigh circumference: measure the fullest length of the thigh above the knees. Measure that from the waist.

10. Additional measurement. Though not required, these measurements can be taken for completeness.

   a. Knee circumference: measure the fullest knee length when the person is sitting or squatting.

   b. Calf circumference: measure the fullest part of the leg below the knee.

   c. Heel-instep circumference: measure the foot from heel on one side to the heel on the other.

Upper Body (for the bodice)

1. Body centers: from the back, measure the bony prominence at the back at the highest level on the level of the neck to the lower edge of the waistline

2. Full bodice length: measure the back, from the shoulder to the waist. Measure the front from the bust to the waist.

3. Full bodice width: from the center back, measure to both scye level sides. From the center front, measure length to both scye level sides. Record the two measurements.

4. Side seam length: Measure from ¾ to 1 inch below the elbow to the waistline

5. Shoulder width: Measure the shoulder from tip to tip, passing through the scyeline in front and at the back.

6. Shoulder slope: `Measure from the center back waistline to the shoulder tip of each side passing through the shoulder blades diagonally. Repeat for the front. Record the 4 measurements.

7. Shoulder length: measure side neck out to the shoulder tip of each side.

8. Chest length and bust contour: starting from the mid-shoulder, measure the contour of the breast until you reach the rib cage on the under edge of the bust.

9. Width of shoulder blade. From the back, at the level of 1 to 1 ¼ inches above the elbow, mark the arm crease. Measure the length from one arm crease to the other

side passing through the shoulder blade. Repeat at the front.

10. Blade and bust tips: measure from the edge of one shoulder blade to the next and from the tip of one bust to the next.

11. Bust and shoulder blade length. Measure from the edges of one shoulder blade to the waistline and record the other shoulder blade to the waist line. Measure the bus tip of both sides to the waistline.

Arms (for the sleeves)

1. Underarm length: Measure from the level of ¾ to 1 inch below the elbow to the wrist line.

2. Elbow tip position: Measure from elbow tip to the wrist line.

3. Overarm length: Measure from the shoulders to the elbow to the wrist line.

4. Biceps circumference: Measure the fullest part of the upper arms.

5. Elbow circumference: Bend the elbow at 90 degrees. Measure from the elbow tip across the crease to the elbow tip again to complete 360 degrees.

6. Wrist circumference: Place 2 finger on the wrist line and measure the circumference at that level.

7. Hand circumference: position the thumb to level with the index finger. Measure the circumference of the hand as it passes through the base of the thumb.

Chapter Summary

In this chapter, I have learned that:

- There are three fitting pattern methods: pinned, trial garment and measurement methods.

In the next chapter you will learn methods of pattern alteration.

Chapter Five:
Methods of Pattern Alteration

There is an art involved in pattern alteration. It involves the customization of the pattern chosen to the specific measurement of the person. From the fitting, you must be able to note all the necessary adjustments either from the pinned, trial garment or the measurement methods. It is not good if the garment you produce will still have a lot of major adjustments once you work on the fabric. Study the measurements of your client and evaluate where they are exactly placed in the pattern pieces. I will be showing you a general procedure for alteration and then the different methods of alteration.

How to Alter

1. Take a look at the big picture. Look at all the adjustments you have to make and how they relate within one pattern piece and with each other.

2. Choose a pattern alteration process that is appropriate. There are three methods you can choose from: slash, seam and pivot.

3. Place the pattern and work on a flat surface, whether it is a board or a reinforced surface. Iron out paper or fabric so there are no creases.

4. Proceed systematically when addressing adjustments.

   a. Start with the length. Make adjustments, either increasing or decreasing the length of a piece.

b. Follow with the width. Make adjustments, whether shortening or widening the width of a piece.

5. Ensure the accuracy of all the adjustments. The final garment must not produce any tension like unnecessary creases, but should look flowing and flat.

Seam Method

The seam method is the safest for beginners. You will now be cutting through the pattern pieces but you will only be manipulating the edges or the seam allowances. You will be cutting the seam allowances from the concerned edge and never the interior of the pattern. The adjustments are quite easy and simple to do. Be careful that the seam allowances you made are clearly marked because they don't maintain their forms in this method. Here are the methods of seam alteration:

1. Locate the concerned stitching line for adjustment.

2. Locate the pivot points on the stitching line. These are areas where there is greatest variation or where uneven and even changes are present.

3. Create clip lines from the edges cutting across the seam allowances to reach the pivot points.

4. Place the alteration paper underneath.

5. Cut the concerned seam allowance.

6. Create hinges to allow movement of the pieces by cutting through the clip lines

7. Make sure that the pattern area is secured to the alteration paper

8. Appropriately change the loose pattern pieces according to the degree needed.

    a. Slide the seam away from the pattern area to increase an even amount of length or width needed

    b. Slide the seam towards the pattern area to decrease an even amount needed

    c. Pivot the seam away from the pattern to increase an uneven amount needed.

    d. Pivot the seam towards the pattern to decrease an uneven amount needed.

    e. If there are even and uneven changes, make the necessary even changes first before the uneven ones. Slide then pivot.

9. Secure the changes to the alteration paper.

Slash Method

When you say slash, you are really cutting through the pattern from the side to the interior. This method involves adjusting the pattern by cutting through the interior of the pattern of the concerned body area, either to increase or decrease the size. This is good if the pattern really needs to be adjusted evenly on one side. This method is quite challenging if you have multiple points of adjustments which are not even. It can be prone to distortion as the biggest adjustment length can overpower minor but important size adjustments. Here are the procedures to accomplish the slash method:

1. Plan adjustments near the edge of the change you want to correct.

2. Create a method for evaluating all the necessary changes in the pattern piece.

   a. If the change is even, you can proceed to extending the line across the pattern

   b. If only one seam line is to be changed, mark the alteration line as it crosses the concerned seam and continue as a straight line. Make another line between the alteration line and the line cutting across the unaffected seam.

   c. If only the interior needs to be changed but not the seamline, mark a line extending from one stitching line to another in the same affected area.

   d. When you have both even and uneven changes, mark the line from the pattern edge of the concerned area and extend. These lines should note when the changes from even to uneven.

3. Form hinges on the stitching lines by putting clips on the seam allowances. This will allow for movement in the parts of the pattern and maintaining its flatness.

4. Place the alteration paper that will mark the area.

5. Cut the alteration paper along the slash lines.

6. Pin and combine the areas you have altered to the unchanged areas in the pattern.

7. Appropriately change the loose pattern pieces according to the degree needed.

   a. Separate the patterns in the same amount parallel to the increase of even length or width needed

b. Overlap the patterns in the same amount parallel to the decrease of even length or width needed

c. Pivot the pattern edge away from the interior of the pattern to increase an uneven amount needed.

d. Pivot the pattern edge towards the interior of the pattern to decrease an uneven amount needed

e. If there are even and uneven changes, make the necessary even changes first before the uneven ones.

8. Pin and secure the final manipulated pattern areas to the alteration paper.

Pivot Method

The pivot method attacks the alteration problem differently from the others. The previous patterns would need to cut from the pattern piece itself, whether the interior or the seam allowances. With the pivot method, only the contour edge of the pattern is altered. You start with making a copy of the area where you want to alter, whether to increase or decrease in size, whether evenly or unevenly. You take this duplicate and place or pivot it on the existing pattern and then retrace the whole pattern, incorporating the alteration. In this way, you don't disturb the grainlines. With this method, you can incorporate a lot of variations of alterations and still come up with a cohesive final pattern. Be careful at marking the new cutting lines because they can be obscured in the final tracing. To avoid this, use a bright ink like red to trace the final outline. Here is the complete process of the pivot method:

1. Indicate the areas in the stitching line that needs to be altered. This could be areas where there are a lot of even, uneven or a combination of both, alterations are located. There could be more than one pivot point in a given area.

2. Use another pattern paper and trace the outline of the pattern area of concern.

3. Create a new pattern edge on the edited pattern.

4. Pivot the duplicate on the original pattern according to the degree of alteration needed:

    a. Pivot the duplicate beyond the original to increase even sizes.

    b. Pivot the duplicate inwards to the original to decrease even size.

    c. Pivot the duplicate away from the original along the stitching lines to increase uneven sizes.

    d. Pivot the duplicate towards the original along the stitching lines to decrease uneven sizes.

    e. If there are even and uneven changes, make the necessary even changes first before the uneven ones.

5. Secure the properly positioned duplicates on the original. Make sure they don't move during the tracing.

6. Trace the new outline of the pattern piece. Mark the new outline with a bright marker like red.

7. Cut the new pattern pieces and mark the new stitching lines.

These three methods are the most common ways you can alter the new pattern. Familiarize yourself with all three because there are some changes that are more appropriate for each method. For example, if there is a greater area of even change you need, a slash method may be more efficient rather than retracing the whole outline using a pivot method. If there are only small changes involved, the seam method will be more helpful. If you have a lot of variations with both even and uneven characters, the pivot method will be more useful. Regardless of method, make sure that the edited pattern is free of tension and maintains the grainline.

Chapter Summary

In this chapter, I have learned that:

- There are three methods of pattern alteration: seam, pivot and slash methods.

- It is important to know which technique is to be used for symmetric and asymmetric changes.

Chapter Six:
Project I: Hands - Alter the Sleeves

Are you ready to begin your alteration projects? I'm sure that with all that you have read so far, you are excited to apply the lessons to actual patterns and fabrics. I have written seven simple alteration projects which you can try. These are the most common problems you will encounter when you begin alterations and so we will start you off with the most basic ones. I have designed each project to tackle a particular fitting problem that you will most likely encounter when you begin receiving clients. I suggest that you do not rush through these projects, aiming for perfection before you proceed. These projects are meant to be enjoyed so take as much time as you need.

The chapters are designed into a structure that will allow you to proceed in a systematic pattern. You begin with analysing the body of your client first and identifying what is inherently problematic with the structure. Next, I will discuss typical fitting errors you will encounter in reference to the body size of your client. Next, we will take the fabric and highlight what needs to be done to address your client's problem. Then we will proceed to a step-by-step process of alteration. Through this method, you will be able to move more efficiently and commit less errors.

We begin with basic bodice patterns. Jackets and sweaters are the typical Christmas gifts of aunts and mothers to teenagers. You will always get a hand-knitted sweater with the most festive colours. The fit on the shoulder and the overall design may be quite charming. Often, it is the sleeves which make all the variations. I have encountered clients with sleeves hanging out from their hands like scarecrows. The usual remedy is to pull the extra sleeves back so it becomes bundled over the arm or the forearm. It can restrict movement and can be aesthetically unattractive. But altering sleeves are one of the easiest projects you can start with.

Analyse the Body

When you encounter arm sleeve alterations, it is good to analyse the entire arm from the tip of the shoulder to the elbow to the wrist line. The growth of the arms is not even for everyone, so we can detect variations of length before or after the elbow crease. In people with shorter arms, the bones of the arms or the forearms may be shorter than average. There are also cases where the hinge flesh which anchors the arm to the torso is formed closer to the rib cage making the entire arm shorter. You have to decide which part of the entire arm is shorter, if it is the arm above or below the elbow. This is where you make the necessary adjustments.

Analyse the Fit

The dart of the sleeve must align with the elbow joint. If the dart lies higher than the elbow joint, the forearm area may be too restricted in its movement because of the tight fabric. But if the dart lies below the elbow, there is more room in the arms which gives an illusion of puffiness or a big volume.

The sleeve hemline must also be exactly at the wrist line. If it is above that line, then the sleeve is too short. If the hemline is beyond the wris tine, it can hide the hand and make it look stubby. So you have to monitor both the elbow joint and wrist level and adjust which part of the arm is most concerned.

Fabric Needs

If the upper arm is bigger than average, then more length is needed above the elbow joint. If the upper arm is smaller than average, less length is needed. This also goes for the forearm in terms of distance from the average. You have to adjust which part that will make the dart coincide with the elbow joint and the sleeve hemline to coincide with the wrist line.

Recommended Alteration Method

1. First, measure the arm circumference and length of the client, as well as the elbow and wrist circumference. Do this for both arms because not all arms measure equally on both sides.

2. Based on these measurements, decide what part of your client's body does not conform to typical fitting standards. It may be that the client has a shorter arm than the forearm. Once you have decided which part of the arm needs to be adjusted, mark the area on the fabric where you want the elbow and wrist line to be.

3. Using the slash method, you can adjust the concerned portion. Cut the pattern according to the adjustments needed. When you are satisfied with the pattern, you can translate it to the fabric.

4. In the case of short arms, you can cut the length of the fabric so that the dart is at the elbow joint and the hemline is at the wrist line.

5. Start cutting the fabric according to the adjustments in the pattern. Give some allowances and then stitch the sleeves.

6. Press the hem of both sides to flatten the sleeves area.

7. Fit the clothes on your client and see if there are minor changes to made.

Chapter Seven:
Project II: Neck - Widen the Front Neckline

There are some shirts or jackets which can choke a wearer because the neckline is too tight. And there are some women who want a bigger neckline to expose flattering neck angles. Whatever it is, the neck can be quite tricky to alter. You have to measure the neck circumference and indicate the areas you want to expose. You have to be careful that the new neckline will allow the wearer to be comfortable but also modest-looking.

Analyse the Body

Try to understand the cause for the discomfort. There are people who have larger neck circumferences than the average person, whether it is because of more tissue deposits in the area or more developed muscles.

Analyse the Fit

When you have a neckline that is too tight, the back neckline rises. There is also a circular wrinkle forming below the front neckline indicating tension in the fabric. The front armscyes may also look larger as the fabric is pulled down. The shoulder blades and chest fitting lines also rise because of the tension upwards.

Fabric Needs

When you have a client who has a larger than average neck circumference, the neck opening must be wide at the sides and low at the center front. In this way, the fabric will relax and the shoulder blades and chest fitting lines will return to their normal position.

Recommended Alteration Method: Slash Method

The goal is to widen the back and front neckline while lowering the front neckline. You can adopt the slash method for this.

1. Measure the client's shoulders, neck circumference and chest width. This will give you an idea how large the neckline needs to be. Make sure that the client can move freely with the new neckline while not exposing intimate parts of the client's body.

2. Create a fitting garment with the appropriate pattern according to your client's measurements.

3. In the fitting garment, cut through the neckline seam allowance at ½ inch intervals in the center front area as needed to widen the neckline.

4. Check if this will relieve the tension on the bodice. Continue cutting until there are no more creases seen.

5. Mark the area where the tension is relieved and then extend the cut sideways until you cover the entire front neckline.

6. Proceed in the same manner with the back neckline cutting close to the shoulder seam.

7. Draw the new neckline using the front and back necklines. Stitch all seams.

8. Iron the neckline and the entire bodice to flatten the clothes.

9. Let the client try the clothes on and adjust any minor changes needed.

Chapter Eight:
Project III: Waist: Change the Seam

There are shirts and dresses which fit well on the shoulders and neckline but look voluminous in the waist area. For bustier models, the overhanging fabric may make them look bigger than they really are. When you have too much fabric in the waist area, the bodice may even extend to the hips and thigh areas. The overall look is unattractive and this would require altering the very waistline of the fabric.

Analyse the Body

Understand what part of the body is not proportional. There are some models who have tighter abdomens and hence, their stomach is jutting out less than the average person. Posture also plays a role. If the person is standing overly erect, almost extending the back, the waistline usually will become smaller. In hourglass types of figures, the waist is considerably thinner than the ribcage and the hips. Their sides are also more sloped and longer from the arm joints to the waist.

Analyse the Fit

The fabric usually crumples or is baggy at the waist area. Vertical folds appear as the extra fabric bunches.

Fabric Needs

You will need to either take out the excess cloth or convert it to details such as pleats or drapes or any stylish detailing. I would recommend decreasing the length of the waist area and let the garment flow more closely to the body contour.

Recommended Alteration Method: Slash Method

The goal is to narrow the side area of the waist. You can accomplish this through the slash method.

1. Measure the client's waist area from the centre back to the sides and the center front to both sides.
2. With the client's measurements, select the best fit pattern and create a fitting garment. Take the fitting garments and place it on a flat surface.
3. Create tucks of equal width on the waistline, both in front and at the back, near the side seams.
4. Distribute the tucks evenly and then cut the excess. Adjust until there is no more tension in the fabric.
5. Taper the tucks towards the armscye seam line. Stitch all seams.
6. Iron the clothes to flatten it.
7. Let the client try the clothes on and adjust any minor changes needed.

If you are going to be altering a skirt, pants or trousers to fit the new waistline, you will follow a similar technique. Still use the slash method:

1. Take the appropriate measurements on the client (waist, hip, leg length, crotch area, hemline).

2. Select an appropriate pattern for the client's measurements. Create a fitting garment based on the pattern.

3. On the fitting garment, release the waistline seam on each side of the seam area.

4. Form tucks on the front and back near the seams until the excess fabric is removed.

5. Make sure that the new pants retain a wearing ease that will still be comfortable to the client.

6. Taper the tucks to the side seams until the tucks disappear. Stitch all the seams.

7. Iron the skirt or the trousers to flatten the clothes. Examine if the new fit is within the structural lines.

8. Let the client try the clothes on and adjust any minor changes needed.

Chapter 9:
Project IV: Chest Alteration - Loose Fitting Garment

There are garments that don't look flattering on the chest area. When you pick out a garment that is too big on you on the chest area, the extra fabric will make you disproportionately more voluminous on the thorax. There are many reasons for this including a smaller upper back, a smaller chest or a flatter bust size. To alter the chest area, you will need to measure all the pertinent bodice or upper trunk measurements we have outlined in Chapter Four.

Analyse the Body

Notice the different parts of the upper trunk. The rib cage may be smaller than average. The upper back or chest muscles may be less developed. The person may also be standing too erect so that the back is flat, which can decrease its size or transfer the fabric to the shoulder area. The distance between the arm joints may also decrease.

Analyse the Fit

When fabric is too loose, the extra fabric hangs loose in the chest, shoulder blade or armpit area. If you raise the arms forward, the armscyes will cut against the arm hinges. If you lift the hands upward, there is less movement as the sleeves are pulled against the arm.

Fabric Needs

You will need to decrease the fabric at either the chest area or the shoulder blades. The change will also affect the scyeline and the armscyes. This will lessen the tension in the area and allow more fluidity in movement.

Recommended Alteration Method: Slash Method

The goal is to cut the excess fabric at the chest and shoulder blade areas. The slash method is recommended for this.

1. Make the necessary measurements on the client (chest width, bust size, bodice length, shoulders, waist).

2. Choose a pattern that fits your client's measurements. Create a fitting garment according to the pattern. Make the necessary adjustments on the fitting garment before you translate it to the fabric.

3. To tighten the chest area, begin by forming a vertical tuck around 1 inch from each armscye.

4. Remove the excess fabric in the chest area until the tension is relieved.

5. Adjust the widths on the fabric until it becomes smooth.

6. Taper the tucks near the shoulder and the scyeline. Stitch all the seams.

7. Iron the entire bodice to flatten out the clothes. Make sure that the new fit is within the structural lines.

8. Let the client try the clothes on and adjust any minor
   changes needed.

Chapter 10:
Project V: Broad Hips - Loosen the Pants

I have a number of clients who come in for alterations because their pants don't fit anymore. This may rather be embarrassing because some of them have really grown, especially in the hip area. They say that they are usually a size 26 but they can't pull up the pants completely to the hips. Or they will try to force the pants through but there is much restriction in movement that they open the buttons to let their waist breathe a little. This rather common problem has a simple solution that can end your clients' embarrassment. It may need a lot of acceptance of their current form but it is possible to still wear your old pants.

Analyse the Body

Measure the hip area again from center back to the sides and the center front to the sides. Compare this with the standard hip size for the persons built and height. People with bigger hips either have a bigger bone structure, or more deposits of soft tissue in the joint area.

Analyse the Fit

When you fit their old pants or a pair of pants they want to fit in, there are creases and tension on the hip area. The rest of the trousers will be pulled up as a result, so watch out for the hemline. Sometimes, the pants cannot actually come all the way up to the hips because it is stuck in the crotch area.

Fabric Needs

You will need to adjust both the width and the length of the pants especially at the hip area. this will also create longer side seams curved near the hipline. When you have more fabric in the hips, the rest of the trousers can extend to the intended length.

Recommended Alteration Method: Pivot Method

1. Make the necessary measurements on the client (waist, hips, leg length, crotch).
2. Choose an appropriate pattern based on the measurements.
3. Calculate for the amount of fabric you will need. This is obtained by measuring the garment you are going to alter and subtracting the sum of the total body hip measurement plus the wearing ease.
4. Now, divide this difference into four to compute for the side seam allowances.
5. Trace the new side seam measurement on the hipline area. Curve back near the original seam line and below the thigh area.
6. If you feel that the legs have also become wider, extend the new line parallel from the original starting point from the hipline to the end of the hem. This adjusts the legs to match the adjustment on the hips. Stitch all seams.
7. Iron the trousers to flatten the clothes. Observe if the new fit is within the structural lines.
8. Let the client try the clothes on and adjust any minor changes needed.

Chapter 11:
Project VI: Short Legs - Trim the Garment

You might like a particular fabric of pants but your legs are too short for the actual length. The usual solution is of course to have the pants altered by a tailor to your desired length. You can do this for yourself or for others if you understand leg measurements and how to trim garments properly. This is one of the easiest projects you can undertake because the process is quite straightforward.

Analyse the Body

The legs of your client may be shorter than average, whether it is shorter above or below the knee. Compare the client's leg measurements to the standard for their height and build.

Analyse the Fit

Sometimes, pants hang too close to the ground and at uneven lengths. If you continue wearing pants this way, the edges may become frayed from too much friction with the ground. A quick fix solution is to fold the pants to the heel length. The fold may look very bulky and, over time, the new edge will also fray, damaging the fabric. The extra length can also cause the person to trip, which is dangerous.

Fabric Needs

You need to trim the garment below the thighline by decreasing the amount of fabric. If there are ruffles or pleats on the edge, you can adjust on the fabric itself or include the details in the shortening. If there are flares on the knee, the adjustment may be above or below the knee level.

Recommended Alteration Method: Pivot Method

1. Measure the leg length on both legs and mark the new hemline on the pants. You want to measure both legs as some clients may have asymmetrical legs.
2. Choose an appropriate pattern based on the client's measurements.
3. Mark the hems of both legs ½ inches from the original hemline to the new one in the front crease. Trim the allowance and see if the pattern now matches the measurements of the client.
4. To translate the pattern onto the fabric, place the pants on the table, mark it with ruler and chalk according to the pattern.
5. Cut the fabric carefully and stitch the hem in accurate measurements.
6. Press it evenly to create the correct crease.
7. Let the client try the clothes on and adjust any minor changes needed.

Chapter 12:
Project VII: Add Pockets to a Shirt

Adding pockets is both stylish and functional. Pocket detailing can add excitement to a bare area and contribute to the aesthetic appeal of the shirt. It is also very handy to put small items in pockets such as keys, money or cards. This dual purpose makes the skill of adding of pockets an important one for any tailor.

If you plan to put a pocket on your shirt, the shirt itself must fit your client well. There are male and female patterns for bodices and these shirts and dresses that must first have been created for you to add the design to. The pockets are just an additional detail and should not distract you from the basics of fitting a good shirt or dress.

Analyse the Body

Understand where the hands can go naturally in a shirt or dress. The usual positions are in the chest area or in the waist. Do not place pockets in areas which are unreachable to the hands or will make the wearer uncomfortable in any way.

Analyse the Fit

The appropriate location and size of the pockets is essential to the aesthetic and functional value of pockets. They should be placed in areas of easy access to the hands. The depth of the pocket must also be appropriate. You don't want a shallow pocket because that will limit its functional capacity. You also don't want a pocket that is too deep because that may look unflattering on a shirt or dress when you have too many things inside the fabric. There are standard sizes according to the fit of the bodice. You can customize your own depending on the measurements of the client, the aesthetic value you are targeting and the functional capacity the client needs.

Fabric Needs

Proper placement and size of the pockets is important. There are lots of pocket patterns available. It is advisable that the pattern in the shirt matches the pocket. They should not clash in terms of colors, textures or pattern. Otherwise, the pocket will stand out which is not the effect you want to go for. Choose an appropriate pocket pattern for the shirt or dress you will add it to.

Recommended Alteration Method

1. Choose the pocket pattern that is most appropriate for your purposes. There are commercial pocket patterns available or you can design your own. Experiment with the kinds of fabrics you have. Excess fabric may be transformed into a pocket if you're feeling creative.
2. Determine the final position of the pocket. For the chest area, choose either the left or right chest area in between the scyeline and the center front. For waist pockets, place them near the hip.
3. Mark the placement of the pockets with pins. Ensure that the pockets are placed symmetrically. A 5 inch opening of the pocket is optimal so incorporate that to the design.
4. Cut out the pocket patterns on the fabric you will be using. Create stitching lines with allowances of ¼ inch.

5. Locate the side seams near the pocket area you have determined. Cut out the stitches on the side seams.
6. Stitch the pocket with a ¼ inch allowance from the edge.
7. Sew the side seams and then iron the side seams. Try the dress or shirt on and allow the client to place their hands on the pockets. The fit must be comfortable, with the opening not too wide and not too small.

Final Words

Congratulations! You should have completed your first projects. Now that you have made all seven sewing projects, you're almost ready to launch your own collection! I hope you didn't rush through as each activity was meant to be enjoyed. Hopefully, also, you were able to apply the standards of fitting and the selection of patterns to guide you in your sewing.

I would advise you to take a picture of your unfinished and finished sewing projects. Take a picture of the patterns you used and the final dress or shirt or skirt you have altered. This will be good for you to document your progress. When you look at the pictures, you can see objectively which parts you may have missed in altering well. You can zoom in on little seam showings or pockets not lying along the structural lines. This is not just about analyzing minute details; it serves as feedback to learn from and build on for your next projects. Don't be careless and think that the client will not spot those little errors. Sometimes, when we are so focused on sewing the tiny details on clothes, we tend to forget the bigger picture. When you take a picture of the finished project, you see how the different patterns come together to make a unified whole. Aim for excellence even if you make mistakes in each project. If you have this goal, then you will work hard to achieve it.

More importantly, I want you to take a picture with each person you have made those clothes for. Make them wear it in your shop. Let them try it on for you. Ultimately, sewing is not just a relationship with fabrics, it is a relationship with real people. Your goal is not to make perfect clothes that look good in a catalogue or in pictures. The goal of sewing is to make clothes for people that fit well and feel good.

This also serves as a reference or resource for you as you take on more and more projects. Document the progress of your alteration by using the pictures of people to help you remember a particular project. When you have a problem with adjusting the sleeves, think of Mrs. Brown who came to you with a lot of fabric hanging around her wrist. What did you do? How did you adjust the length? Instead of focusing on the measurements, you get to remember the person and then the recall becomes better and you have a template to work from. When you catalogue your work, you are actually making your own portfolio for other people to see just how good you are.

In the introduction, I told you about my peculiar way of asking about a client's main problem. Instead of asking, "What do you want me to do?" I asked my clients "What look do you want?" This simple rephrasing of the question launches conversations on body size and family stories, on dreams and aspirations. I would like to end with my own way of closing a project with clients. Some tailors would leave the finished project in sealed bags and let the customer pick it up and the payment seals the deal. If further alterations or tweaks to the existing alterations are needed, the customer can always go back and have it fixed in a jiffy. Contract ended. I find that too mechanical and rather abrupt, not to mention inefficient. With a transactional manner of dispensing projects, the lack of communication will make the clients unnecessarily come back and forth to get the fit right.

My technique is to invite the client to try the clothes in the shop. I prefer that the client take some time to try the clothes on where I could see them and I can make instant alterations. I give them space to change and let them put on the newly-altered clothes. The moment they walk out of the changing room, you know that you have made a good project based on the way the clients carry themselves. Invite them to look at themselves in a full-sized mirror. Allow them to take a look at how the clothes fit them, from one side to another. Let them move in the clothing, exploring positions which may cause tension, feeling how the clothes will fit when they are sitting or walking. Let them feel how a well-fitted set of clothes should feel like. Give them a moment with their new clothes. And then ask them finally, "How do you feel wearing this dress or shirt?" It is the reply to this question that will affirm your vocation as a tailor.

Some of the memorable replies were: "I feel very tall when I put this on" or "I feel very beautiful and elegant in this dress." I feel giddy inside when some people with poor posture suddenly try to match the clothes they are in by adopting a better stance. Others can't help starting at themselves at the mirror. I take that as a compliment any day. When people begin liking themselves in the clothes they wear, I feel that I have done a good job.

These subtle effects show us that clothes are not just fabrics that we put on to cover our bodies. Clothes should help reflect who people are inside. If you don't feel confident, put on a well-fitted shirt and pants and let that help you reach that confidence you need. If you feel you are too small, let a well-fitted set of trousers give you the extra height you need. Ultimately, as tailors, we are not just changing clothes; we are changing the people wearing those clothes.

When you end a project this way, there is a 100 percent assurance that the client will come back to you. When you touch them in a profound way, through the emotions, they appreciate it. They feel that their opinions are valued and that you aren't just there for the money. You begin establishing a relationship with your clients and word will spread very fast. They are going to recommend you to their families and friends, to their coworkers and superiors. Before long, your shop is going to compete very well with my business. Establish these relationships because you will be seeing these people for a very long time.

My final advice to you is to sew, sew, and sew. Keep making new projects because that is the only way you are going to learn. You will become better at cutting the length of trousers if you do it over and over again. One good trousers alteration is a lucky accident; making well-fitting trousers again and again is a sign of mastery. Once you get better at the basics, you might try your hand in intermediate difficulty projects which I will be teaching you in another book. Remember to keep sewing. You shouldn't let a day pass by when you don't trace a pattern, stitch a seam or simply handle fabrics. The hand has a way of remembering so you cannot be an occasional alterations tailor. Practice, practice, practice!

It is also a good exercise to observe people. When you are sitting in a park or riding on the subway, try looking at people and their clothes. Learn to spot good-fitting clothes and those that aren't. Observe what clothes are becoming trendy, and how people move with their clothes. In this way, you are extending your shop to the entire neighbourhood.

I hope you enjoyed this book and I look forward to meeting you in succeeding projects. I think tailors should learn from other tailors because we all share that passion for people and what they wear. Keep on sewing!

Intermediate Guide to Pattern Fitting and Alterations

Introduction

On one level, finding any piece of cloth to cover the body might be said to be easy. But putting together clothing that properly identifies, presents, and makes an individual feel comfortable and proud requires some creativity and professionalism. The art of modern pattern fitting and alteration aims to make something outstandingly unique out of a simple already-made cloth or a plain fabric.

There are so many reasons why clothing is important. It might be for modesty, comfort, presentation, or plain survival. The kind of clothes you put on your body would, firstly, be judged by how they fit you. Anybody can try on any clothing, but they most likely won't try on something that doesn't fit.

Most of the time, our preferences for what fits our bodies are affected by what we feel most comfortable in. This is where individualism comes in. Every cloth or pattern will not be suitable for everyone. In most cases, eight out of ten persons would require a unique fitting for their clothing. You would have to consider the shape of the individual. Commercial pattern makers work with pre-existing models and structures, but we all know very few of us meet those standards. As such, drafting the right pattern for the right fit for an individual means that you have to consider every curve and mold on the individual's body, and the usual idea is to flatter the right places. Being able to alter patterns and create new fittings also makes individuals feel unique in their own right.

This is the art and the essence of the sewing industry. Basically, if you can't get the patterns to fit, then, most likely, your finished product will not come out right. Those who have started out in fashion have to see that making patterns is one of the most challenging parts of sewing, but a good pattern maker makes a great designer, hence a great sewer. There are those who have started down this road, and then they feel like this path might be too cumbersome for them. You might not want to go through all the mathematics and measurements involved in creating your precise fitting. Then it is not too late for you to change course. The devil is in the details. You would have to go through the steps outlined in this book and create what is needed for you to become a great pattern fitter and alteration expert. In this guide, you'll notice that we place more emphasis on patterns to enhance your designer approach.

A career is not built in a day; it is built over time based on your works and your reputation in the industry. The goal of this guide is to equip you with what it takes to create a pattern that fits with the mind of a designer. The bottom line is making something better out of whatever fabric or simple dress is in your hand. Also, don't forget that beauty is in the eyes of the beholder. Your intention should always be to make something that looks better on a person wearing the clothing, something that is properly fitted and which accentuates their body.

Of course, there are commercial patterns available for general clothing, but you may want to create unique pieces for designs and improve on already-made clothes. Perhaps you want to make something bolder out of already existing designs. If so, this guide is for you.

If you haven't already done so, I would ask you to read my companion book, the beginner's guide to pattern fitting. You'll see in that the basics of pattern-drafting and sewing constructions.

In this intermediate guide, we'll be diving deeper into a semi-advanced level of pattern making, fitting, and alteration. I'll show you examples of how you can get creative with making patterns and alterations. We will touch on some beginner's points as a reminder, but will mainly focus on advanced-level methods to show you ways of how to create patterns with expertise and creativity. You will learn how to manipulate patterns into the perfect fit and draw up your own designs in the process.

This guide covers all the requirements, the use and application of tools and equipment necessary for pattern fitting and alterations. There are many cases where the inability to use the right tools and methods to effect an alteration has been the reason why the end result has gone wrong. Without the right tools in your tool kit, and the knowledge to use them, the results will almost certainly be mediocre. This book will also help you understand the different types and methods of pattern-making and alterations.

We will also be looking into a step-by-step process of how to redesign some simple garments. This will give you hands-on knowledge about how to creatively make your pattern designs.

We will look at how to;

❖ Redesign a man's long shirt into a woman's beautiful dress.

❖ How to combine two different colored tee-shirts into one.

❖ Alter your low waist jeans into a high waist.

❖ Make a simple pattern of male trousers.

❖ Create a blazer pattern.

❖ Create a lady's blouse pattern and experiment with sleeves.

❖ Create collars.

At the end of the guide, you should be able to use the step-by-step processes to alter patterns and make new fittings without changing the structure of the clothing.

→ You will know the right tools to use to create perfect patterns and alterations.

→ You should be able to know the different pattern types and pattern methods. You will also be able to know the best ways to apply the pattern methods and what kind of designs are best produced with the different pattern methods that are available.

→ You should be able to create pattern fittings without damaging material or changing the overall measurements of the clothing.

→ You should be able to make professional alterations, understanding the different methods of alterations to create perfect fits. You will be able to use the right alteration method to ensure you produce the perfect piece at the end of the day.

→ You should be able to create your unique designs through alterations and pattern fitting.

Chapter One:
Tools, Equipment, and Accessories

The best pattern creations are made with the right tools and equipment. Not having the necessary sewing tools is like not having the necessary ingredients needed to prepare a meal. Without the right ingredients, that meal won't come out the way the menu described, and it definitely won't taste how it should! No designer would want that result for their proposed idea.

Why are the right tools for pattern fitting and alteration?

1. **Fabric texture/characteristic**: Fabrics are sensitive materials that are factored around precision. Fabrics are designed and made with different textures, designs, and aesthetics. Some fabrics are soft, while others can be hard, stony, or even very light in weight. Using a tool made for a hard fabric on a soft fabric can cause irreparable damage. This could mean more cost for you and time wasted.

2. **Design implementation**: There are some patterns that can only be made when you have specific tools. For instance, to start with block pattern making, you have to get your cardboard or papers handy. If you don't start this correctly, you can make errors, therefore causing damage. You end up losing your fabric and your time.

3. **Alteration precision**: The best alteration methods can only be carried out with the right tools. Failure to use the right tools can cause damage to your fabric, and, rather than making an alteration, you would end up disfiguring your clothing. For example, tools like

seam rippers help quickly loosen the seams and not expand the thread holes.

4. **Effectiveness**: Using the best tools and the right tools ensure that you save time, avoid damage, and consequently save money. For instance, pressing tools can help straighten fabric properly to avoid squeeze, hence helping you make better patterns quickly. Imagine you are the only pattern maker in your design outfit, and you needed to churn out a considerable number before the end of the day. Or, you have a forthcoming event that you must make a dress for. In cases like this, the last thing you would need is a scanty tool bag. The right tool will help you make the most of your time and ensure that you have the kind of quality that you want to put out there.

5. **Durability**: Your tools will last longer when you have all the right tools present at your work table. You might wonder how. This simply means that you won't have to use the wrong scissors or needles for the wrong fabric. Using the wrong ones might mean that you would most likely damage your tool and still be unable to get your desired result. You would be incurring more costs than you thought you were saving.

6. **Safety**: The importance of a safe working environment cannot be overemphasized. Imagine walking into your sewing store, only to be pierced by a needle in your foot. That could mean no work for you on that day, to say nothing of the pain and inconvenience. Only the right tools and equipment can help ensure that you avoid occupational hazards.

Your work table should have the following categories of tools;

→ Cutting Tools

→ Marking Tools

→ Measurement Tools

→ Pressing Tools

→ Needles

→ Sewing Equipment and Accessories

Cutting tools

Cutting tools are, obviously, a very important part of your pattern making. The kind of cutting tool you use will determine how clean your cut will be. It also affects how fast and smooth you will be able to cut. You can make straight cuts, curve cuts, and angular cuts with these implements.

- • **Angled fabric scissors**: They help you make cuts in long and single strokes. Especially when cutting heavy fabrics. They increase your effectiveness.

- **Micro Serrated scissors**: These scissors are great for lightweight materials, especially if you will be working with satins and crepes. They have micro-serrations on the blades to help you hold material firmly to avoid slipping.

- **Paper cutting scissors**: Paper cutting scissors helps you make your pattern on cardboard or paper. This helps keep your fabric scissors as sharp as it should be.

- **Small sharp fabric scissors**: This cutting tool is great for cutting and trimming seam allowances. You can also use it for cutting small motifs for appliques.

- **Duckbill Scissors**: These scissors are specially used with your applique needlework. They help you clip out extra fabric from your work. The paddle-shaped blade helps you cut clearly around your applique stitches. They easily pick at the threads between your work.

- **Pinking shears**: Pinking shears have a zigzag edge that makes them easy for you when finishing your fabric edges. This prevents your edges from fraying and unraveling.

- **Bent scissor**: The bent scissors are designed to have a bent lower blade; this helps keep the blades parallel to the table to help you cut your fabric with more precision.

- **Spring-action scissors**: Spring-action, as the name implies, are scissors that are fortified with a spring; hence, it makes it easier for you to open the blades and cut. This way, you are faster, and you also have less stress on your fingers and wrist. They're great for sewers that might have arthritic or related conditions.

- **Double curved embroidery scissors**: These scissors fit perfectly in embroidery hoops. The blades can easily get into the hoops and tight spaces, making it easy to make cuts during embroidery.

- **Thread Snips**: This tool helps with cutting threads when doing embroidery. It helps you cut out threads easily while sewing. You can get the one that gives you a rope to hang around your neck.

- **Rotary cutters**: Rotary cutters are very effective for cutting heavy materials or more than one material in layers at the same time. If you work with many materials at once, then the rotary cutter will be a very important cutting tool for your work kit. Thick fabrics like faux, felt, vinyl are best to use it with.

- **Buttonhole cutters**: As the name indicates, this tool gives you clean button cuts. Gone are the days where you have to use your scissors to make holes that might be too big or cause damage. Use a buttonhole cutter to make a hole by placing the chisel in the center of the buttonhole and push it down sharply between the thread.

- **Seam rippers**: A seam ripper is a must-have tool, at least if you get on your tailoring table a lot. You can cut open threads easily without damaging the fabric. They help rip the seams off without causing any damage. This is a must-have tool if you're making alterations.

- **Exacto knife**: This helps you make smaller holes in fabrics.

- **Awl:** This tool is useful for feeding gathered fabric into the needle.

Measuring Tools

When it comes to pattern-fitting and alterations, we could say that if 'measurement' is king, then 'cuts' might well be the queen. Using measuring tools helps you transfer the right measurements and make the right adjustments where necessary. Without great measuring tools, you'll be spending a lot of time going back and forth on your work because of significant changes that you might have to make.

- **Measuring tape**: Measuring tape is a must when it comes to tools for sewing. The measuring tape helps you take body measurements, and you can also bend, curve, and wrap the tape to take the kind of measurement you want. It's then easy to transfer this to your cutting paper.

- **L-scale**: Also called the tri-scale. It is mostly made of wood or steel. It is mostly used to draw perpendicular lines or drafting on brown paper. It helps to draw accurate lines. Mostly 90-degree angles and straight edges, it measures, rules, and squares jointly.

- **French curve**: Drawing and cutting smoothly is one of the arts of professionalism, and your French curve ensures you get it right. When it's time to blend in the lines or draw a perfecting smooth curve, then you can lean on the French curve.

- **Clear Ruler**: A clear ruler will help you draft patterns and add your seam allowances.

- **Meter ruler/yardstick**: You can use this to draw lines and create hemlines. You can use this to check for grain lines. It can be metal or wood.

- **Hemline gauge**: A hemline gauge is very useful for your sewing project. It helps you create hems by folding the hem of the fabric as deep as you want it to go. It is made of metal that does not rust. It has markings to measure the space or length of the hem.

- **Buttonhole gauge**: A button guide helps you discover the size of a button to make better holes.

- **Flexible curve**: This is a curvy plastic rule. It is a terrific tool as it can bend to fit whatever shape you want. You can draw curved or straight lines with this. It can be adjusted to fit lines to draw your patterns. Whether straight, curves, or arcs, this is one tool that makes your work really easy.

- **Grading ruler**: These rulers are used to grade patterns by placing the rulers around line curves.

- **Folding ruler**: These are used for pattern measurements and are best when you have a small tool kit. That's because they're foldable and easily stored.

- **Seam gauge**: A seam gauge is used for measuring button placement, hems, waistbands, and more. This is a useful tool in sewing. If you have been sewing for a while, you will know how handy a seam gauge can be.

- **Metric conversion charts**: This tool helps you convert body measures from imperial conversions to metric conversions and vice versa.

Marking tools

Marking tools helps you easily make notes of alterations on your fabric and take note of points you want to come back to. They help you make lines for cutting and sewing.

- **Tailor's chalk**: This is used for marking your fabric. You can transfer lines, mark pattern lines, make lines for darts and cuts. Tailor's chalk comes in different colors. It's intended to rub off the material. However, some materials with special kinds of colors might not be suitable for using tailor's chalk.

- **Disappearing pens**: These pens are also used to make your marks on fabrics for cuts. You can find them in some craft stores. They are designed so that the ink will evaporate after a certain period of time.

- **Tailor's tack**: This is one of the oldest ways of making markings. But it is most effectively used for marking your darts.

- **Tracing wheel**: This tool has multiple teeth; the teeth can either be seated or smooth. It can be used to make slotted perforations. It's also used to transfer markings onto fabric from fabric. You can use tracing paper with this tool or not. Markings that might be best transferred with a tracing wheel include darts, pleats, buttonholes, notches, and placement lines for applique or pockets.

- **Carbon paper**: Carbon papers are essential in pattern-making to prepare patterns and keep them for later use. It helps you make alterations to your pattern without ruining it or causing any damage.

- **Soap**: Soap is used to mark out patterns in sewing and pattern making.

Pressing Tools

Pressing tools help smoothen fabrics to enable better cutting precisions. Some tools are fabric-specific, while others are more effective for smaller areas. The following are pressing tools.

- **Steam Iron**: An iron is very important because it helps flatten out every bump or ridge.

- **Pressing Cloth**: A pressing cloth helps you form a bridge between your pressing iron and your fabric. It is normally a cotton cloth that is placed on the fabric. The iron plate then goes on top of that.

- **Ironing board**: An ironing board is vital for the pressing process.

- **Clapper and the point presser**: This is a tool used to flatten edges, especially for seams, pleats, and darts.

- **Seam roll**: A seam roll is an essential tool used for pressing out curvy edges. It works well in pressing out seams, darts, and zippers.

- **Tailor's Ham**: The tailor's ham is an effective and handy tool used for pattern-making when pressing and molding seams, sleeves, caps, and darts.

- **Sleeve Board**: This helps you increase your precision in pattern-making. It is a small board used for ironing that helps you iron the sleeves all around the edges without having to crease or spoil them. It helps you save space and does a better job of pressing your sleeves.

Sewing Equipment

Your sewing equipment ranges from your sewing machines to items that help you manage and maintain your sewing tools.

Sewing equipment includes;

- **Pincushion**: A pincushion will help you keep your pins in one place, so you can easily pick them up when you need them and replace them when you are done.

- **Bobbins**: Bobbins hold the thread installed below the needle in the sewing machine; they produce thread for the bottom part of your stitch.

- **Presser feet**: This is a useful piece of equipment. It is used to install zippers or insert piping or beaded trim. It holds one side of the material on one side of the needle to enable you to sew.

- **Duster**: Dusters are used to clean crevices in your machine. One will normally come with your sewing machine.

- **Thimble**: This little bucket-shaped tool helps you push needles into your fabric without having to hurt your finger. This way, you can be fast and precise.

- **Screwdriver**: A screwdriver is very handy for when you might need to dismantle a part of your machine that requires cleaning or repair.

Sewing needles

Sewing needles come in different types and sizes. There are hand sewing needles and machine sewing needles. The kind of fabric and type of thread are some of the things that affect the needle that you'd use for your project. Weightier fabrics will require larger sizes of needles and vice-versa.

- **Ballpoint Needles**: A ballpoint needle works well with knits and will slip within the fibers rather than piercing through them.

- **Stretch needles**: Stretch needles are designed to sew elastic clothes like spandex, synthetics, suede, and swimsuits.

- **Denim/jeans needles**: These needles are made for the heavy and thick stuff. They are reinforced to go through these thick layers of fabrics, and you won't have to bother about your needle coming out in one piece.

- **Leather Needles**: These needles are better used for leathers as they have chiseled points to cut through tough substances.

It's always best to use the specific needles for the proposed fabric type to avoid damaging your fabric and spending time replacing needles because of breakages.

Other accessories include:

- **Erasers**: Erasers should be kept together with your pencils to make corrections where necessary on your cardboard and paper.

- **Pencils**: Pencils always come in handy. You'll need them to draw your design sketches on your notepad and make drawings on your cardboard or paper where necessary. They're useful for taking down measurements and notes if you are one of those that prefer writing with a pencil.

- **Table**: Getting a flat surface for your sewing can help you make better patterns and take away a lot of distractions that come with clutter around you. To focus and do better work, you will need a table where you can put your cardboard or fabric down.

- **Glue**: Glues are terrific, especially when making patterns from cardboard and papers.

- **Tissue paper**: Tissue papers are an essential accessory in your tool kit. You can easily use them to wipe away dirt when needed. They always come in handy.

- **Cardboard notepad**: Having a notepad is essential to record all your measurements and keep them in one place. Measurements are the maps of your patterns and design. If you don't have them, you're like a traveler losing the direction of their course.

Maintaining your Sewing Tools and Equipment

1. You should oil your sewing equipment to prevent rust.

2. Keep your tools in their cases or packs if they are not in use. If you do your sewing at home, keeping your

tools safe also means safeguarding them from young children, and, in some cases, adults. If your home is like mine, then I can tell that there will be those people who want to breeze into your workspace to use your fabric scissors to cut a piece of paper or their hair. Your equipment is your livelihood, so make sure it's not accessible to other people.

3. Wipe your blades and other equipment clean with a damp cloth when they are dusty or dirty.

4. You can use sewing machine oil to do your oiling. Oiling your blades is a great way to keep the hinges working fine for a long time.

5. You can also sharpen the blades for maintenance when you feel like they are dull.

Chapter Summary

- Using the right tool is essential for creating amazing designs.

- In this chapter, we've provided you with a list of must-have tools you need to make your patterns.

- Learn to care for your sewing tools using these simple tips.

In the next chapter, we will dive into how to identify and make different types of patterns.

Chapter Two:
Methods of Pattern Fitting and Alteration

This chapter will be divided into two subjects, and we're going to discuss Pattern-fitting and Alteration. Pattern-making depends on various factors like gender, age, and regionality. Suitable measurements and study of basic garment patterns are of great help in creating novel designs. There are basic garment pattern garments which have been commercialized over time.

What is Pattern Making?

Pattern-making is the building block of your design. It forms the framework of what you have to sew. It's like the bridge between your idea of a design and what will be eventually constructed. Pattern making starts with drafting the pattern. Patterns can be drafted on any kind of material. However, cardboards are first used for ease of use and other benefits.

When starting a project or, for instance, when cooking, you would need to have an image of the kind of food you want to cook. Let's say you want to prepare pasta. You know how your pasta looks and tastes on a plate. You plan to make it look that way. Next, you would have to list the ingredients you need to purchase to make your pasta. After which, you purchase the ingredients and clean them to make them ready for cooking. Making your pattern is pretty much getting your ingredients ready for your cooking.

Pattern making is laying down the template of the idea or design that you have first drawn out on paper. This is dependent on the kind of design you have put down. Just as the ingredients will be dependent on the kind of food you are making.

Importance of Pattern Making

Why all the fuss about pattern-making? The arts of sewing and fashion design have evolved over the years. But something that remains very crucial to sewing is the fundamental step of pattern-making and fitting. Before we delve into the types and methods of pattern-making, here are some basic important points.

- **Achieving the right fit:** As we have established so far, the crux of every made dress is the fitting. Hence, the importance of fitting cannot be overemphasized. This is the first important reason why we create patterns. It's because you have to achieve fit. If it doesn't fit, you would have to make it fit.

That is why creating patterns is so important. They help you achieve fitting. The body has different molds and curves, and the idea of designing clothing is to come with your unique design that should fit into those molds and curves. To do this, you would have to create something that aligns. Your design and the body form must match. This is where pattern-making comes in. A comprehensive fashion designer should also, ideally, be a great pattern maker.

- **Reducing Error:** Imagine cutting through an expensive silk fabric after taking some measurements, only to find that you have made the cut some inches too small and you haven't made the right curves at the arm areas. There is no going back on this. You can try to correct your errors, which will very likely only lead to more errors, or take out another expensive silk fabric to begin again. There will be neither the time nor the funds to cover your wastage. Pattern helps to reduce errors and save a massive amount of time. This is further understood when you see that you can easily replicate what you have already done on another fabric.

- **Duplicating style:** Pattern making helps you duplicate style for mass production. It can also help you add to a style by carrying out alterations without redesigning from scratch. The whole process is a wonderful way to save time and money while creating perfectly fitted clothing for individuals.

Different Types of Pattern Making

There are different types of patterns. A sloper pattern or a block pattern is a pattern that is already made. These patterns are available for purchase for home or commercial use. Most people that prefer more individually creative designs for a person or style might not find using a sloper or a block pattern is the best option. But, when learning, it is best to use these patterns as they form the fundamentals of your design knowledge. And they help you understand the aesthetics of your pattern-making. Hence, you see the faults and possibly where you can add or improve upon.

The block or slope pattern is developed for everyday wares or clothes that are standardized. Bespoke designers and fashion houses would rather design their own patterns from scratch for their customers.

You may have a dream of starting your own commercial fashion line; maybe you want to open a line of female blouses or men's shirts. Where there might be already available commercial patterns for these, it is unethical to use these commercial patterns if you are going to start your own fashion line. It is something like an unwritten law.

Most of the time, fashion houses will normally hire their own pattern-maker to create patterns for them. Most outfits have at least one pattern-maker employed just to design patterns. The goal of understanding and using the pattern types is to help you understand the fundamentals.

Factors Affecting Pattern-Making

The factors that affect pattern-making generally influence why we choose the kind of clothes we wear. This is important for a designer to take note of because it will determine the type of pattern to use and the method of pattern-making to apply. Let start with:

Age: There are size differences that come with age, especially when you are talking about large variations like adults and infants. The age of an individual, or a group of persons that you might be designing for, can largely affect the pattern. Infants, for instance, might not do well with a sharp dart or an elaborate design. The elderly might not do well with a standard waist-size or waist-cut. This must be considered when making your pattern.

Climate: Climate also affects pattern-making; not only will you have to consider the kind of material that will be used to sew your design, but you'll also have to consider if a pad might be used in certain areas of your production. You might need to allow for more or less seam space.

Figure: The figure of an individual also has a large role to play. For pattern-making methods that restrict the size of the individual the cloth is being made for, you should strongly consider the size of the individual before starting out on your pattern.

Methods of Pattern Making

There are different methods of making patterns: the flat-pattern method, as you might guess, involves the pattern being drawn up on a flat surface. This is the most commonly used method. Other methods like Flat Pattern making, Pinned pattern method, Trial Garment Methods, and Measurement method are also sometimes employed.

Flat Pattern Method

The flat pattern method is the making of patterns on a flat surface, just as the name implies. It involves drafting out your patterns with the measurements you have taken on cardboard or papers.

Measurement tools like rulers and curves are used here. It will also involve the use of tools like the awl, drill, and notcher. The flat pattern method is mostly used to create block or sloper patterns for simple garments. This method is usually made out of paper or cardboard, and does not need to allow for seam allowances. It is mostly used to make basic apparel, especially men's outfits. To become a very skilled pattern-maker, you will have to get proficient with the flat method. It's an excellent way to acquire the fundamental skills. It really is the basis of pattern-making. With this method, you can easily manipulate and alter your design. It is easier to increase size or add to design.

Basic Tools Required

- Flat Surface/Table of standard height

- L-scale

- French Curve

- Ruler

- Pencil

- Measuring tape

Pros of the Flat Pattern Method

- It makes altering patterns easier from your already cut-out basic pattern.

- Commercialization is easier with this method because you can grade your patterns to different sizes with the same basic pattern.

- You can easily redesign an old pattern.

- Most people going to mass production of clothes will normally use flat pattern due to its ease of grading.

Cons of Flat Pattern Method

- The flat pattern method requires professional training because of its standardized basics. You will need to have perfected the art to be a flat pattern-maker.

- Flat pattern method is a 2-dimensional approach; as such, it does not give you a full picture of what your design looks like. It is difficult to imagine the complete nature of your outcome until you get there. Therefore, it is not recommended for complicated designs.

- To make a basic sloper pattern, you will require a full knowledge of pattern and pattern-making.

Pinned-Pattern Method

The pinned-patterned method involves draping a muslin mock-up pattern directly on the form. This is also called Draping. It is a more advanced 3-dimensional form of pattern-making. In this method, you would need an appropriately-sized model to be a form for your pattern-making.

Muslin is a lightweight cotton cloth. This is draped on the form and then pinned on the required areas for your pattern. You can reuse muslin for more than one pattern. Also, this method helps you get a full picture in advance.

Pinned-patterns are mostly used to construct more complicated forms of design, but using a pinned pattern would still take you back to working with your dotted-paper. At the end of the day, before you can work with a drape for a pinned pattern, you would still need to know the basics of flat pattern.

How to drape (The Pinned-pattern Method)

Draping is simply placing a muslin material over your form. Set out all the tools and materials you need, and follow the next steps to create a pattern using the pinned-pattern method.

What you need:

- Muslin

- Disappearing pen/pencil

- Scissors

- Pattern-cutter

- Glue

- Pins

- Dotted paper

- A form

- Tracing Wheel

- Hip curve

- French Curve

- Tape Measure

❏ **Step 1- Set aside your form/model**: The form you set aside should represent the kind of pattern you would be making. For instance, if you're making a pattern for a women's skirt or a basic bodice, you should have a whole form for both patterns. If you have a form that starts from the waist for the women's skirt, or you have a form that ends at the waist for a basic back bodice, you should also have forms that will reproduce this. In this guide, I will be taking you through the steps of making a pattern for a basic bodice.

❏ **Step 2- Place your Muslin on the model**: Take a piece of the muslin material and place it at the back of the form. Spread it out, starting from the neck down to below the waist area, then use a pin to firmly hold the muslin to the model at the lower part of the neck. The pin should not be pushed straight into the model; it should be pushed toward the right side of the model to firmly hold your muslin in place. Continue to place the pins in the areas you want your material to cover. You can cut out the end parts of the material that are obviously not in use on the area. Use your pen to mark out the arm area, the neck, and the dart line.

❑ **Step 3- Cut out the extra material**: Cut out all the extra materials that are not part of the marked areas. Take out your marked muslin. This material is now used to make a pattern using your dotted paper.

❑ **Step 4- Trace your pattern:** Place your dotted paper on the flat table and place your muslin on the paper. Pick up your tracing wheel and run it on the marked lines on your muslin. You can run it over again, maybe twice or thrice, to be sure that it has been properly traced on your dotted paper.

❑ **Step 5- "True" Your Pattern**: Now that the pattern is traced on the dotted paper. You will have to "true it." Truing your tracing is simply making your tracing bolder and better. Take off your muslin on the dotted paper. This is where your French curve and your clear ruler are useful. Use them and a pencil to draw on your tracing. Use the French curve for the arm area and other curved areas.

Your pattern is ready for use.

Considerations when draping

- Remember to retrace using your tracing wheel until visible traces are noticed.

- Use a pattern cutter for a smoother cutting process.

- Use a disappearing pen or chalk that you can wipe off from your muslin, just in case you might want to use it again.

- When drawing in your darts, you should true it by half an inch down from what you had mapped out from your pattern.

- Allow for seam lines when trying your pattern.

- Do not allow for a seam line at the center on your bodice.

Pros of Pinned-Pattern Method

1. You can easily modify your design or style while you drape.

2. You have a clear visualization of your design and what to expect at the end of your production.

3. You can truly express your skills and be very creative with your patterns.

4. There is a more precise fitting using this method.

Cons of Pinned-Pattern Method

1. It is time-consuming.

2. It is expensive.

3. You cannot eliminate the use of a form.

4. It cannot be used for commercial production.

5. It is mostly better used for designer clothing.

6. It requires different sizes of dress forms.

7. It requires lighter materials for draping.

Measurement Method

Also known as the Drafting method, this involves taking measurements of the individual that the cloth is being sewn for and cutting out drafts based on the measurement. You simply draw your patterns on paper based on the measurements that you have taken. Hence you have to ensure that you take precise measurements. A Block or Sloper can be utilized for a pattern draft. Basic blocks of patterns can be used from drafting, which includes bodice back, bodice front, skirt front, skirt back, and sleeves. These blocks can be added upon to create better designs.

Considerations when drafting

- Drafting should be done on a flat surface after the measurement has been taken.

- You should also carry out your drafting on the wrong side of the material.

- You should use the same size of paper required for the garment measurement.

- Ensure you use your French curves to make accurate curved lines.

- Distinguish back and front with different types of lines.

- Use your tailor's square to draw right angles.

- Well-sharpened pencils should be used for accuracy of lines.

Tools Required

- Paper (brown sheets)

- Pencil

- French curve

- Clear Ruler

- Measuring tape

What to consider when taking body measurements:

- **The posture of the individual-** Ensure that the person is standing erect when taking the measurement.

- **Remove all outer garments-** The person should take off any outer garments, especially jackets and coats that might alter the precise measurement that you intend to take.

- **Use quality tools-** Ensure you are using a quality standard measuring tape.

- **Round measure-** Take care to take round measurements in the arm areas, neck, and others. Don't let the tape be too tight or too slack.

Pros of measurement method

- A good draft can be easily graded to any size.

- You can easily get creative with basic blocks to get other designs for your choice.

- A draft can be stored up and used again and again.

- You can easily make corrections on the paper draft before cutting on the material.

- Wastage is less.

- It is inexpensive when compared to other methods.

Cons of Drafting

- It doesn't exactly fit all since the slopers are normally made based on the individual's body measured.

- A basic draft has no seam allowance but only ease; hence seam allowance is to be marked on the fabric.

What are Alterations?

Alteration is merely the act of making a change or modification on a garment or a pattern. In this section, we will be talking about pattern alterations.

Pattern alteration is adjusting a pattern to fit. There are many reasons why adjustments and alterations are often required in pattern making.

Most patterns might have been bought commercially: Commercial patterns are normally built with standard body sizes and frames. If you are one of those that buy commercial patterns for your production or for your personal use, then you will definitely need to understand alterations.

People want something unique: Whether you are designing something for yourself or for someone else, the chances are you might want something slightly different from a basic pattern or clothing.

Difference in body shape: Difference in body shapes can make you alter your own pattern, especially if you want to replicate the same pattern for another clothing for someone that might have a slight difference in size. Or, you may just want to alter the fit for yourself.

Difference in clothing preference and shape: You might have gotten tired of an old garment or style, and you want to redesign it to make something different; alterations would be just the thing that you need.

How I wanted to alter my trouser pattern

I'm a working mother, and I'm sure you can imagine the effort it takes to balance personal needs, my career, and my family. Honestly, one of my major personal goals has been to go back to having a flat tummy! Even though I am not exactly fat, I am just so psyched about a flat stomach. Oh, the shame I feel when I can't take in that bulge! It ruins the picture I would imagine in my mind as to how I want my clothes to look on me. But being who I am, I still try to hide it as much as I can with corsets, and the right pair of trousers. Sometimes, though, nobody wants to stifle their breathing or bring an amount of discomfort on themselves just because they have to wear a tummy trainer. That's why, if I ever get trousers, and they're not high-waisted, I have to alter them to my perfect fit, because that is the only way I can be comfortable in my clothes. Now, don't think I have thrown exercise to the wind, but it's just I haven't had the time! So, for now, I have to trust fitting my clothes to do my body trick for me, at least when I am all dressed up.

Importance/ Principles of Pattern Alteration

- **You should alter your pattern before cutting a garment**: Fitting alteration is important because once the fabric is cut, alteration or changes made are limited to the seam allowances and the darts on the garment. If you have a small allowance proportion you will be unable to carry out major changes on the garment; as such, you might be constrained to losing the already cut material.

- **Keep a record of pattern alterations**: Keeping record of pattern alterations is also important to help you go back to previously made changes or provide an opportunity to track the changes you have made.

- After a standard pattern alteration is done, you will observe that:

→ The designer line and design are preserved unless the design is purposely changed.

→ Changes are not obvious, and they do not affect other areas of the pattern.

→ The pattern remains flat and does not lose balance and proportion.

→ The grain lines are retained.

- **Corresponding patterns should also be altered**: The same pieces on the pattern must be altered to ensure that they correspond with the alterations of the major piece. For instance, the alteration made on your back bodice block should also be done on the front bodice block.

- **Add extensions with tape or glue**: Increases in length or width that have been added are made by taping or gluing the extension material (pattern tissue) to the original pattern.

- **Share the same structure as the original piece**: The altered pattern should have the same structure as the original pattern piece.

- **New altered pattern should be a flat block like the original pattern**: Ensure that your newly altered pattern retains the flat shape of the original block. This is because your block might tend to change in shape or fold if you don't follow the right principles or methods.

- Proper movement on altered lines to ensure that the altered line is the same as the original line.

- Ensure that you make slashes, folds, and adjustments parallel to the grain line. That is, parallel to the center front line or the center back line.

- When it comes to length and width, ensure that you make corresponding changes. On the other hand, this might not apply for alteration that has to do with increased bust area increase.

- Tucks and darts used to make width proportions smaller should be half of the actual amount removed.

- If an adjustment of the width is to be made when it comes to waist measurement, then divide the measurement to be added into two. And add the half-inch on one part of the pattern block and the other half on the other part.

To ensure that you have made all the right adjustments, here are some ways you can check your pattern to be certain you have made the right fit. You can use your mirror to check the adjustments before cutting your garment to ensure it is the right fit by placing it and the material area on your body or a form.

- → There is adequate ease for moving, sitting, and bending.

- → Grain lines that are crosswise are parallel to the floor.

- → The arms seam curves smoothly over the shoulder.

- → The crotch depth area is not too tight or too binding.

- → The darts made are pointing to the fullest parts of the curve made.

- → The hemline is even.

- → Your hipline is well fitted.

- → The side seams, center front, center back, and the lengthwise grain lines should hang straight or at right angle proportions to the floor.

- → The pants' legs hang smoothly and do not restrict the leg.

- → The waistband stays in place on the waist and fits when sitting and bending.

- → There is no excess fabric around or across the front or back crotch level.

- → The sleeves sit well, with no wrinkles.

Methods for Alterations

There are several methods. While it is almost impossible to achieve a perfect fit for most clothing without alterations, carrying out alterations with the wrong steps or the wrong way will cause a lot of problems for you and your fabric. Doing alteration the wrong way can lead to:

→ Wastage of fabric

→ Increased cost

→ Ruin of entire design and pattern

→ Waste of time

→ Dysfunctional design or dress

Fit is important to make garments achieve perfection, but sometimes perfection is subject to other factors. Here are some of the keys to a good fit:

Perfect measurement: Taking correct measurement is the foundation of all things. When taking measurements, try to ensure that it is done accurately.

Some best measurement practices includes:

Ensure that the individual stands up straight and looks forward at the time of the measurement. It can be a bit tricky taking floor-length measurement, particularly if you are taking it on your own body. So, if you are doing this for yourself, try to stand in front of the mirror and use a tape measure that you can simply allow to drop down and hang. This way, you don't have to bend to do your measuring.

When it comes to the breast area, our breast shape can vary in size when we are wearing a bra or not wearing a bra. If you are going to wear a bra with the finished garment, then take the measurements with you wearing a bra. Likewise, if you won't be wearing a bra, then leave it off when taking the measurements.

Trend: Trends, or the fashion outlook for the time, might be a bogus trend or a more eased-out pattern. This can be seen with tee-shirts or sweaters. Its style is not to hug the frame of the body, yet there must also be a fit to it. Hence, the pattern and alterations must fit the design that the trend is made for.

The elasticity of the fabric: This factor also affects alteration and is also looked at in our next chapter, "Fundamentals of Apparel Design." Alteration points will change depending on the type of fabric. You might need to allow and disallow an inch or less, based on the kind of fabric that you are using to make your finished work.

The amount of ease needed: Individuals might want different things in clothing production, especially when it comes to bespoke clothing. A standard way of making your design alteration might not play out when a person wants more room on her garment. This also means that this factor should be put into consideration when making alterations.

Size and type of figure: We all know that most of our bodies rarely fit into the standard image of a model. And when it comes to bespoke clothing for yourself, it can affect your pattern. Some persons might have more thigh proportions and more arm proportions than you would find in a model form. This makes alteration necessary. That might also affect other aspects of the pattern that has been designed. Taking this into account will help you choose the right alteration method. Commercial patterns are often prepared from standard body charts, so alteration on those patterns, if you want a bespoke fit, is inevitable. The methods of alteration might involve folding out excess areas to make the pattern block smaller. Or cutting through patterns to increase size and overlapping to decrease or increase dimension. Or by redrawing placement of dart and seams.

Below are the detailed methods of carrying out alterations.

Seam Method

Alteration using the Seam Method works great for adjustment on the seam lines and altering just along the grainline. Using a seam method works well if you are trying to adjust areas around the hip or waist for skirt, trouser, blouse patterns, and more.

It is quite easy to implement and allows you to make the changes on your pattern paper that you need so you can keep using it again and again. We will look at some simple steps to using the seam method in altering a pattern.

Material you need

→ Tissue paper

→ Your pattern to be adjusted

→ A pair of scissors

→ Some transparent tape

→ A clear ruler.

❏ **Step one**: Place the pattern on a flat surface, then identify the areas where you want to make alterations.

❏ **Step two**: Identify the pivot points. Remove the seam line. To expose the grainline, cut the pivot points to allow just enough to make a hinge.

❏ **Step three**: Place cardboard or paper underneath the area if you are making an additional adjustment.

❏ **Step four**: Then, you add the inches that are measurements that you intend to add to it. If you're making a reduction alteration, you can measure the area you will be cutting out, then when it is cut out, you can add your seamline back to your pattern by taping it back to the pattern.

Pivot Method

Also called the Pivot and Slide method, It is also a great way to make your pattern alterations. It focuses on working around the grain lines and allows you to make adjustments both on the width and length of your garment. I will be using a blouse pattern to show you how to use the pivot alteration method. In this project, we will be making alterations along the armhole. Most times, some standard blouse patterns might not conform to an individual's specific size, especially when it comes to the arm area, even when everything fits. Using Pivot for this saves the day.

Material you need

→ Tissue paper

→ Your pattern to be adjusted

→ A pair of scissors

→ Some transparent tape

→ A clear ruler.

→ Pins

❑ **Step one**: Place the pattern on a flat surface. Identify the areas where you want to make alterations. Place a pattern tissue underneath the pattern block that you are altering.

❑ **Step two**: Take the extra measurements that you will be adding and divide it by two.

❑ **Step three**: Use your pin to place it at the shoulder point where you will be taking the alteration from. When the pin is at that point, you can slide the pattern paper back and forth as you want. But do it just enough to measure out, and then mark the points of adding on your tissue.

❑ **Step four**: Join the points that have been marked with your pen or pencil.

❑ **Step five**: You can simply use glue to add your pattern, and it has been successfully adjusted.

You can also use the slide method to adjust the length of your basic pattern block. Add your new measurement and mark its points on the end of your tissue just beneath the pattern block. Simply slide the pattern block up to draw out and join the points that you have marked.

In pattern alteration and fitting, getting the grainline and structural line right is very important. After making or adjusting your pattern, this aspect of the pattern must be strongly considered to keep the fit in place. Using these methods of alterations ensure that your grainline and structural lines are in place to give your garment the actual design look it should have.

Chapter Summary

- Patterns are important in sewing because they help make sewing so much easier.

- There are several kinds of patterns; understanding types and methods of pattern-making is essential to making better clothes.

- Knowing the importance of alteration, and the many methods of alteration, will help you better understand why it is necessary to the sewing process.

In the next chapter, we will discuss the fundamentals of cloth design.

Chapter Three: Fundamentals of Apparel Design

In apparel design, for you to create amazing designs and be at the top of your game as a designer, you must be willing to understand the concept of all areas of design and sewing before you can even begin. It's easy to think that a designer is one that simply sits down and drafts up creative illustrations for clothing on a notepad, but this is not the case. A designer would have to go through these fundamental steps we will be discussing in this book to have the kind of work that would produce successful clothing.

This chapter seeks to help those ready go through the process of understanding what it takes to create your own concepts, bring to life your own designs, and successfully showcase them to the world. As an alteration expert, you need to understand the methods of pattern-making, designs, and alterations. To make great alterations, you should understand design fundamentals.

These are fundamentals that affect everything. Without these basics, you might end up creating things that are not relevant or suitable. Remember that as a designer, what might appeal to you might not be appealing to the average person. While you might care about the details of your creation, like how you have managed to use a food theme to create a jumpsuit, someone else might only care about its fitting and trendiness.

As Vivienne Westwood said, "Fashion design is almost like mathematics; you have a vocabulary of ideas which you have to add and subtract in order to come up with an equation right for the times."

One of the strong factors that significantly affects the design we make is the trend. Historically, apparel has evolved to what we have today with each culture and age leaving its own little mark. So, how do you make your own design that someone would want to wear?

What *is* apparel? Apparel is clothing. Therefore apparel design is simply the act of designing clothing. This can range from garments, underwear, accessories, swimsuits, sportswear, and mostly whatever is worn on the body. As in all art forms, and also what we have always stated throughout this guide, it's vital to go back and understand design elements and principles.

Conceptualization of your Apparel Design

Developing your ideas for fashion should start with what you are designing, and who it's intended for. Well, if you are designing for yourself, the bridge might be quite narrow for you to cross, as you can simply do exactly whatever you have in mind. But, if you are conceptualizing ideas for a person that is not you, or for the public, you have to do much more.

Trends go as fast as they come, and trends are often not fair. Most fashion industry greats have gone on to set the trends over time. But how did they do this? What is a trend?

A trend could be defined as an aspect of popular culture - what everyone is doing now. To begin your design conceptualization, you must consider the trends, and if you want to set the trends, you should consider what makes them. Movies and shows are some of the things that have set trends socially. For example, the Moulin Rouge movie that influenced catwalk and fashion a few years ago.

You have to research fabrics, and read fashion guides and magazines to see designs from others. You can also learn from apparel design experts by studying about their works to understand how they conceptualize their designs. Some fashion firms sponsor their designers on trips to visit places to observe culture for inspiration. For a designer, absolutely anything can be an inspiration, and they should always be on the lookout.

They are always eager to see and feel something that might lead to a great creation. Some great designers have called singers or actors their muse, the person they gain inspiration from. You should always take your notepad with you to record, to draw, and take pictures when necessary.

Some people conceptualize with a theme. That approach creates a space with some boundaries, but where they can experiment with ideas that reflect the theme.

Creating your designs can be by drawing them or illustrating them. Designs are the foundation of a finished garment. Conceptualizing implies thinking about the design, and then you try to detail it with an image.

Drawing can be a difficult task, but just as in all arts, you must start with putting your first stroke down. You should preferably get a pencil and eraser for this. You may have a brilliant concept in your head, but if you never put it down on paper, we will never know if it would work or not!

Instead of worrying about the fact that it hasn't formed totally in your mind, you should go ahead and draw out the little bit you can imagine. If you have taken the first step of research correctly, then this won't be a problem. Your first draft, even if it's very raw, might form the basis for your best design yet.

What is the Difference between Illustration and Drawing?

Drawing simply portrays the schema of the clothing, while illustration creates an ambiance around the schema or structure of the design. This way, someone can know if the apparel can be worn in the summer or winter or how best you designed the outfit to be worn. You also get to know if this is for a lady in an office, a student, or just a teenage girl having fun. Illustrations can convey all these qualities.

This also brings us back to why researching is so important. When you know what matters in the industry, you can know if what you are doing has been done before. It also becomes easier to draw inspiration from already existing products. Many designers have drawn inspiration from military uniforms, for instance. Don't miss any opportunity to put down those strokes when an idea comes to mind.

Sketching Skills for Fashion Design

In drawing your design, it is important that your sketch portrays all the right proportions that you're trying to communicate. Not all of us are the best artists. But we can get better at it when we know a few steps and what to do exactly. Ensure you get a sharp hard pencil and a large blank notepad. You might also want to get some colored pens, but they're not vital, and you can usually get by without.

Scribbling something on paper and not getting it right can be a little disappointing. If you are like me, then it can make you feel like you don't belong in this design world after all. At least, that is what I felt when attempting to get through fashion school. I had a lot of ideas in my head, but I just didn't know how to translate them. I would be asked to try something, but I'd keep out of the way and hide behind others. There are people that are naturally confident with designs, and it almost feels like they were born for it, but that wasn't me. I wasn't a natural, and I mostly felt like the underdog. Nonetheless, I saw that, while it's effortless for some people, all I needed was practice, and I would be able to do well.

As with all industries and aspects of life, practice makes perfect. Talent is great, but it's not always enough; we all have to work at it. All skills and tactics possess steps and principles to getting things done. The underlying rule is that once those principles are put to work, you will get the expected result. This understanding gave me a foothold in my skill. So, you don't have to feel like you were born for this. If you put your mind to it, you can learn anything and be a professional at it.

It's the same thing with drawing; you can become good at it with these few steps.

You should start with creating a croquis on your notepad. This is a notepad model for your design. Some people would prefer getting on with their sketch without one. But this will help your design have form. You can draw a croquis that is standing straight or posing. Drawing one before sketching your design on it also helps you get the dress points right. A pose is often preferred, or even one that is kneeling. Whatever you think is appropriate and useful is fine. You should ensure that your lines are faint at this point.

Follow these simple steps to draw a Croquis

Even if you are bad at doing the sketches, these steps will help you draw out a pretty good croquis. Adding in your cloth sketch will become much easier.

What you will need

→ A clear sheet of paper

→ Sharp pencil

→ A ruler (A clear one preferably)

❑ **Step one**: Draw a straight line in the middle of your paper from the top to the bottom leaving small spaces on both ends.

❑ **Step two**: Divide the straight vertical lines drawn into nine places.

❑ **Step three**: Draw little horizontal lines on the line to mark the figure's areas.

❑ **Step four**: You can put little labels down and name them as follows; 1- Head, 2- Bustline, 3- Waist, 4- Hips, 5- Thighs, 6- Knees, 7- Calves, 8-Ankles. (These labels would automatically form what you draw at each of these points making it easy for you to form your croquis.)

❑ **Step five**: First, draw the head, making a circle on the first area from the head line above. Next, you draw the shoulders just below the head. Next you make a little horizontal line to draw the bustline, and, if you like, two small cups indicating bust.

- ❏ **Step six**: Draw out your waistline at the two ends to the point of the hip line and draw it down to your calves.

- ❏ **Step seven**: Next you make two circle points at your knee point, the calves point, and the ankle point.

- ❏ **Step eight**: Next you mark your crotch, just below the hip line. Draw two lines out from the crotch point to meet up at the ankles. You can draw some shoes at the floor point.

You can make out points for your eyes, nose, and mouth. Then, shade in some hair for your model.

When you are done with your croquis, you can now go ahead to draw your design clothing on it. You can also draw up your cloth lines by placing a transparent drawing sheet over the croquis sheet. On this sheet above it, you can easily see your croquis, so you can draw a better sketch of your dress or design on the form. That helps you make the right outlines that you need to make it what it should be.

Draw with faint lines and only begin to double your lines when you are sure that what you have drawn is what you want to be represented. This is so you can easily erase the pencil line if you get it wrong.

Once you are sure of your lines, you can begin to redraw your lines to emphasize your drawing or make them bold. Once this is done, you have created your perfect sketch.

Elements and principles of design

Elements of design

Elements of design are the basic qualities and aspects of the design process that form the ingredients of fashion. The clothes you are about to make are supposed to flatter people and make them ready for an evening ball. The different elements of design help you make proper design choices that would ensure that, while designing an apparel for an individual, you can focus on how to use these elements in the best ways that help enhance and flatter their best physical attributes.

Imagine trying to make designs for two different people with two distinct sizes. There is a slim petite lady and you also have a tall big lady. Your job is to make beautiful dinner gowns that would make them look stunning for the night. As you start on your design, you would have to first draw out your form and consider how this form would impact the look of your persona. You can think of sharp edges and round curves for your designs.

But the elements of design would help you understand who is better suited for a round curve and who is better suited for a straight edge. You can also consider bright colors, but you would also understand which element is better suited for a dark color than who is better suited for a bright color. Ever wondered why Adele likes black? Maybe that's just because her designer knows what's best for her. Remember that the goal of design is to flatter the best parts of the persona.

- **Form**: Also called the shape or silhouette, it is the comprehensive outline of your apparel. This forms how the whole garment is seen. This creates the total impact of what the garment is and what it represents.

The shape of the apparel is meant to compliment the shape of the individual's body or compliment their best parts. It is the form of the clothing that you notice when it is being looked upon. It is the form that tells you if the person is wearing a jacket or a shirt or a gown. The form is very important. Some aspects are the type of fabric and method of design and construction on the shape or form of your final garment. The shape of garments continue to evolve as trends change to further and better highlight the form of an individual.

> **Line**: Lines are visually expressive. Lines can make a person appear shorter, taller, slimmer, or fatter. Edges are important; these edges can be both within and without the clothing but they are significant in how the garment is seen and formed.

The lines on an apparel are seen as the cuts and seemingly style lines that are created when making an apparel. These lines often work as the element of your design that creates the kind of visual impact that one might see in a dress. Lines on an apparel can make the individual look thinner or fatter. Or you have some features of the body being flattered more than other areas. Lines create shapes like you have for your pleats and darts, especially when it comes to design patterns. It creates more visuals for the blouse then you find on a basic bodice.

Lines can be curved, straight, and structural. Whether diagonal, vertical, or horizontal, these all fall under straight lines. Straight lines work to decrease or increase width or height. Straight diagonal lines that are short are normally seen in jackets, or bell-bottom trousers; the lines would decrease the width of your apparel.

Curved lines will add to the fullness of the apparel. While a curved line adds to the roundness you are trying to portray in a design sketch, when used to illustrate your folds, a more flattened out curve on the apparel gives the body more form representation therefore is considered more flattering. Rounder curves would make your apparel appear fuller.

Structural lines are those kinds of lines that make up the form or structure of the apparel. The structural lines that appear on most garments are the darts and the seam. This is responsible for the fitting and structure of the apparel. There are order lines that are mostly designed for decorative purposes but these are not structural lines. These can be made just to accentuate a certain style or area of the apparel.

- **Color**: Colors are one of the most important elements of a design. They translate to the perception of the finished garment and can influence body structure when mixed with texture. However, on their own, colors can be used as one sees fit with respect to the design and other characteristics. Color describes how fun or cool the apparel looks.

➢ **Texture**: The texture of an apparel is the perceived nature or quality of it. People can use different sensory organs to perceive the structure. You can decipher with your eyes that someone is wearing a satin fabric, for instance. The texture of an apparel largely influences the apparel. This represents the hardness and softness of a fabric. A fabric that is soft or light will drape differently than would a heavy fabric. This is why fabric like satin would fall more easily on the body than leather or thick clothing.

A satin fabric would also show the edges of the body more than cotton fabric would. Hence, you would discover that an older male, for instance, might not feel most comfortable in clothing made from satin. You would also find that there are fabrics which hide the brightness of colors that other fabrics would bring out. If you had a bright blue crepe, it would come out differently than someone wearing a satin blue. You can begin to imagine that bright-colored satin clothing would look a lot more flattering on a slim person than a chubby person.

Design Principles

Design principles are the ideals that help you and guide you in the application of the element of the design. In Apparel design our goals are mainly to accentuate the best physical aspects of the person, achieve reasonable comfort for the person, and improve and portray a beautiful physical appearance of the individual. Using design principles as a guide would help you use your elements wisely in ensuring that you achieve these goals.

- **Balance**: The balance in a design can be asymmetrical or symmetrical. An asymmetric design means that the design is not balanced on both sides. This means that the weight of the design is not evenly distributed at both ends. This can be seen on a dress where there are different cuts at the ends of the skirt.

An example might be a short-long design. Symmetric apparels are normally seen in a formal apparel where there is an even cut at both ends, so we can say that the fabric is evenly distributed. Designs can also have emphasis where you have created a focus in certain areas of the design. This can bring more attention to that area, while also removing attention from other areas.

- ➤ **Rhythm**: Rhythm in a design is created where there is a flow with the colors and the cuts on the design. This can be best seen where color patterns are well-distributed. Or, in cases where different kinds of fabric are used, it is well-distributed and is balanced across the apparel. This also applies for the distribution of the lines used for decoration.

- **Unity**: Unity of design is achieved when one can see that design all falls into place as one. Each part of the elements come together to create and portray one single effect , theme, or style.

Fabric and Technique

Having an understanding of fabric types and the nature of fabric is very important. The fabric you choose will affect the drape, the fitting and comfort of the fabric. This in turn affects the general turn out of your fabric.

Getting used to as many fabric names and characteristics as you can will help you choose the right fabric that best portrays the effect of the design you want to put out. For instance a heavy material for pleats would come out different than a lighter material. Fabrics also affect the fit of your design a lot.

Whatever you are designing, you would strongly have to take into account the kind of fabric. Some fabric stretches. As such, when designing your pattern, you would have to take that into consideration. Fabrics that stretch would fit differently than fabrics that don't. You would have to account for the stretch when taking your measurements. This is typically seen on denim jeans and on leggings. Even though they both fit, they do not have the same area because the leggings have a stretch characteristic. If the leggings were designed with the same size of pattern as the jeans then perhaps it would look poor on you.

The fabric will have an affect on the technical aspect of your design.

> **The Opacity**: Depending on the fabric you use, you may require a lining to bring out the desired result you expect from your production. Also if it is a sheer fabric, you would need a lining to reduce transparency. This would have to be taken into account when stitching and preparing your pattern.

> **The kind of stitches and seams to be used**: If the fabric stretches, or has more weight, you would have to use a stitch that gives more to avoid thread breakage. You would also choose a different kind of stitching for a stronger hold depending on the weight of the fabric.

> **The size of your garment:** Some fabrics are narrower than others. The size of your garment would make you want to lay your fabric side-by-side to accommodate required size if it is a fabric with narrow width. This might also affect the size and nature of your pattern. Hence, it is advisable to understand the kind of pattern you would be using when designing before creating your pattern.

> **Shrinkage**: Shrinkage mostly happens after the clothing is made. And some fabric will shrink with time. If you require ironing during your pre-production process, it might end up getting folded or squeezed in some areas.

> **Fabric handling**: The kind of fabric would also affect fabric handling if you are doing a commercial production. Even when it is a bespoke outfit, you would need to set out handling processes that would

ensure you don't donate the fabric. Also, the right tools should be used to avoid breakage or wearing out of tools.

Textiles

Textiles are made from a combination of thin threads, or yarns or filaments or fibres that are either obtained naturally or artificially or a combination of both. They are made by weaving, knitting, or felting. Combining is interlocking these lengths of fibers or threads in different prescribed patterns to make up a cloth used for sewing. The different properties of fiber affect the final product of the cloth made.

- Silk: Silk is made naturally from silkworms. There are a lot of other animals that produce silk, for textile production it is mostly made from silkworms. It has a long history through countries like India and China. It is known for its soft and durable nature. It is the strongest natural fiber in the world. Silk continues to be a popular fiber because of its cultural and historic heritage. There are now synthetic alternatives for natural silk, but silk is still naturally harvested in some parts of the world. It is mostly used for blouses, nightgowns, evening gowns, and the like.

- Cotton: Cotton is a natural fabric. It is a textile made from the natural cotton plant. It is an insoluble organic compound. It is harvested and spun into yarn, which is then woven into cotton fabric that creates soft cotton clothing. Cotton is commonly the first choice when it comes to fabrics for bedding, underwear, and everyday apparel because it's soft and affordable. Linen is made from cotton.

- Damask: Damask is a fabric with patterns that are woven and not printed on. The designs are achieved with the use of satin weave. Damask fabric can be made with different textiles like satin, linen, wool.

- Cashmere: This is a type of textile obtained from natural sources. It is known for its softness and comfortable feel. It is a type of wool made from cashmere goats and pashmina goats. It is very fine and soft to touch. Mostly, it has a light feel like silk. Sometimes it is blended with other types of wool to give it a heavy feel.

- Canvas: Canvas is a type of textile that is plain-weave made out of heavy cotton yarn. It is a sturdy hard textile. It is known for being durable and strong. It can become a strong outdoor fabric and even water-resistant when you blend cotton with synthetic fibres.

- Chenille: Chenille can be made from materials like cotton, silk, wool, or rayon. Chenille is also the name for the type of yarn used.

- Crepe: This is a fabric that was traditionally made from silk, Crepes can be thin, thick, or lightweight; they mostly look like they have a crinkled dull surface. They are used for evening gowns and some home decors because of how they drape. It is also made from silk or wool or both; today, it can also be made from other synthetic fibers.

- Linen: This is a lightweight and extremely strong fabric. It is made from the flax plant. Linen dries faster than cotton. It is a breathable fabric, and is used to make inner linings of clothing on jackets and other garments. However, it wears out with washing and ironing. It has poor elasticity hence it wrinkles quickly. It is easy to clean. It is more biodegradable than cotton.

- Satin: Satin is a weave that is used to create many kinds of fabrics. Fabrics that are characteristic of satin weave are mostly also called satin or have names accompanied with satin. Satin is used to make nightgowns, lingerie, men's underwear, and also pointe shoes for ballet. If satin weave is used with filament fibers such as silk, polyester, and nylon, the resulting fabric is known as satin. It is a rather soft, shiny, and glossy fabric on its front and has a dull looking back.

Chapter Summary

- Never forget the four basic elements of design. They are the foundation on which you learn to make your first cut.

- The three principles of design discussed in this chapter will guide you in the application of the elements of the design.

- An understanding of the different types of fabric available will help you learn to work with other materials. You should be able to make the right patterns for a cloth if you know how these materials act and respond.

In the next few chapters, you will learn how to make some patterns.

Chapter Four:
Project I – Redesign a Man's Long Shirt Into a Woman's Beautiful Dress

In this first project, we are going to start with redesigning a man's long shirt. There is so much you can do with alterations when trying to design old clothes or already made clothing. This project is not intended to restrict you to this form of redesigning; rather, it is just an example to help you try new ideas.

Using a man's long shirt to be transformed into a woman's dress, we can redesign this into a halter neck gown or an off-shoulder dress, or a plunge neck dress. We can basically do whatever we want with this shirt and have very few restrictions. (Note that depending on your design, you might have to add more fabric to achieve what you have in mind.) In this project, we will be making a plunge-neck women's dress with a waist belt. Let's get started!

Tools needed:

→ A sewing machine

→ A meter rule

→ A pencil or any other marking tool

→ A pair of scissors

→ Some pins

→ A man's long shirt

If you already have a sketch of what you want to achieve, then that would be fine, but if you don't, then you might want to draw a sketch of what you want to accomplish. Then, you can follow the pattern in achieving that design. So, if you do, then your design should be in front of you in the same way that I always have mine in front of me.

- ❏ **Step one**: Your long shirt should be dressed in a form, but if you don't have one, you can simply wear it in front of the mirror and begin to take your markings. First, you take your pencil and take your markings on the arm/sleeves of the shirt. You mark how far you want the sleeves of the shirt to get to.

- ❏ **Step two**: Cut off the sleeves of the shirt at the line that you have marked.

- ❏ **Step three**: Normally, you would take the shirt and place it on a flat surface. If you had placed it on a form, you could simply do all your alterations on the form. Next, you use your pencil or tailor's chalk to mark around the collar and the area you want to have the plunge of the neckline. Then, you make your cutting along that line.

- ❏ **Step four:** You bring the sleeves you have previously cut and cut out vertical pieces of fabric from the sleeves. They will form the waist belt that is about to be made.

Once you have cut out all these, you're ready to start making your woman's long dress. Turn out your dress and put it back on the form. Then, you fold along the line you have cut, just little folds, and begin to use your pins to tack around it. You will do so for the arm area, and for the neck plunge area. Take your pinned-up fabric to the sewing machine and start sewing the folded areas. Once you are done with this, take the cut-out fabric for the belt and sew round the edges.

Once you have done this, you are ready to try on your plunge dress with a waist belt on. You can also decide to add hems to the sleeves to decorate your dress further. Congratulations! You have successfully transformed your man's long shirt into a woman's beautiful dress.

Chapter Five:
Project II – Combine Two Different Color Tee-Shirts Into One

In this next project, we will be combining two different colors of tee-shirts into one. Plain tee shirts are boring, so we want to add some fun to it. This project is a very fun one, and it's a great one to embark on if you are just starting with alteration projects.

You can put together pattern print shirts of two different patterns, or put together stripe shirts of two different stripe colors, or also to try out just plain-colored shirts together. This project is very flexible, and you can choose to do it for male or female tee-shirts. Whatever kind of shirt you choose to work with here, these steps still will work effectively for you. Let's get started! In this project, we will be putting together or combining two different color tee-shirts into one, and two different collared striped shirts into one.

What is needed?

- → Sewing machine

- → Pair of Scissors

- → Seam ripper

- → Pins

- → Rotary cutter

- → Tailor's chalk

- → Two shirts to combine

❑ **Step one**: Get the two shirts that you would want to combine. You should ensure that the shirt is of the same length and width as the other one. You might want to do something that has the same designs on it or maybe try alternate designs. If you would be doing a shirt with a collar, as in the striped collared shirt we are doing side by side, you would also need to get a collared shirt with the same length and width as each other.

❑ **Step two**: For the tee-shirt, all you have to do is fold the shirt into two equal parts right at the middle and cut in between from the neck to the bottom. Do the same for the second shirt. For the collared shirt, you would first need to use your seam ripper to rip the seams at the collar to take the collars off the shirt.

You would need to remove the collars for the two shirts that you would be combining. Then, you turn the shirt to its back and ensure it is equally folded into two to start cutting. Ensure that you get a straight line.

❑ **Step three**: Both for the tee-shirt and the collared shirt, bring the two different parts together that have been cut, alternate them into the back side of the shirt, then use your pins to pin up the shirts to hold them together.

❑ **Step four**: Once you have held them together, then you can take them to your sewing machine and start sewing.

❑ **Step five**: For both shirt edges, you can decide to do an optional zigzag sewing on the edges of the shirt where you made the center cut for durability of the clothing before placing it on the flat surface to start pinning them together. After this, you can head to your sewing machine to sew together the fabric you have pinned together. Once this is done, your tee-shirt is ready to go. But for your collared shirt, there are still a few more steps to take.

❑ **Step six**: Take your sleeved shirt and fit into the collar of the shirt. You can choose to take any of the collars of the shirt you most prefer. You can also decide to take out the pocket from the other shirt and place it on the alternate one.

There you have it! You should have successfully combined a two-colored tee-shirt and a long-sleeved collared shirt into one garment.

Chapter Six:
Project III- Alter Your Low Waist Jeans to High Waist

This next project is one of my favorite projects to do, especially as a DIY project. In this chapter, we will be altering low waist jeans to high waist jeans. If you've read some previous chapters in this guide, you'll understand that I tend to go for high waist jeans!

High waist jeans are so much more comfortable, especially for people like me who do not do so well in the flat tummy area. Even for those who have terrific figures, it's always a great way to enhance your hips curve and accentuate your slender waist. The high waist look effortlessly flatters your figure. Now, let's get started altering your low waist jeans into high ones.

Materials you need

- → Sewing machine

- → Seam rippers

- → A pair of scissors

- → Measuring tape or a meter rule

❏ **Step one**: Spread out your low waist jeans that you are about to adjust into high waist jeans. If you have particular jeans which you would like your low waist jeans to be like, then you can also spread out those jeans to take a measurement from them.

❏ **Step two:** Take the crotch measurement from the already existent high waist jeans and record it.

❏ **Step three**: Rip out the seams on the crotch line of the low waist seam. You can simply rip the threads out until it gets to a considerable length where you know that your already measured crotch length will get to.

❏ **Step four**: Straighten the areas you have loosened. Then, you take the measurement to check if it's the same with your already recorded measurement for your high waist. Cut out the extra areas you have made. Be careful not to cut too much, so it doesn't become too tight.

❏ **Step five:** Once you get the exact measurement, use tailor's chalk to make that point. Then you use your pins to hold the seams, back and front of the length you have opened up.

❏ **Step six**: Begin to stitch it up.

Once you've stitched it up, then you have successfully redesigned your low waist jeans into high waist jeans. Go ahead, and put them on to be sure they fit you perfectly.

Chapter Seven:
Project IV – Make a Simple Pattern of Male Trousers

Trousers are one of the most common clothing essentials, especially male trousers. There is almost no male on earth without at least a pair of trousers. This gives you a good idea how popular they are. However, they can be a bit tricky to create. Making patterns for trousers takes a bit more care than your basic pattern making.

You can think of tight trousers like skinny jeans, or you can think of trousers like plain trousers. Or possibly just well-fitted pants. Whatever your specific need might be, you can tailor your male trouser pattern to look exactly like what you want them to be with these basic steps we will be sharing. Let's get started.

Materials you need:

→ Pattern paper/ dotted paper

→ Scissors

→ Pencil

→ Measuring tape

→ Curved ruler

→ Pattern master/meter rule

→ Clear rule

→ Glue/tape

❏ **Step one**: Spread out your pattern paper or dotted paper on a flat surface. You should either cut out an amount of paper that you know will be sufficient for this project based on the measurement or size of the individual or form that you have taken. Or, simply roll out some of your paper and only cut after you have taken measurement.

❏ **Step two**: Take measurements. These are the following measurements that you should take;

I like to streamline the measurements to take in making trouser patterns into two.

- *The horizontal measurements*

- *The vertical measurements.*

For the vertical measurements, we start out taking the measurements from the waist.

Use your measuring tape to take measurements for the following areas,

→ Your waist down to your hip.

→ Your waist down to your crotch (also called the crotch depth measurement). This is taken from your waist to the end of your bottom when you are seated.

→ Your waist to your knee

→ Your waist to your ankle

For the horizontal measurements, we start out taking the following measurements:

→ Your waist measurement, by wrapping the tape around your waist.

→ Your hip measurement (the tape should be placed around the middle of your buttocks region).

→ Your knee measurement

→ Your ankle measurement

❑ **Step three**: Write down all your measurements because you need them to draft your pattern.

❑ **Step four**: Make a vertical line on your pattern paper using your pencil. Then, make another horizontal line joining it at the top.

❑ **Step five**: Mark out your waist to hip, waist to crotch, waist to knee, and waist to ankle.

❑ **Step six**: You can either use your clear ruler or pattern master for this. Place your clear ruler on your vertical line and mark out (use your pencil to simply shade or tick the area) the measurement you have taken off your waist to hip area. This would be the area from the top of your waistline at the top of the vertical line to where your measurement of your waist to hip line ends. Also, mark out your waist to crotch, waist to knee, and waist to ankle in the same way.

❑ **Step seven**: Place your clear ruler horizontally from the vertical line where you had earlier marked your hip point and draw out a horizontal line to mark out your hip measurement line. For instance, if my hip measurement is 7inches, I will draw out a horizontal 7 inches from the beginning of the vertical line to where 7 inches ends. Also, draw out a horizontal line to mark your waist measurement (your waist measurement is the line that you drew at the top. Hence, it is already drawn. All you have to do is to mark it), mark your knee measurement and ankle measurement.

❑ **Step eight**: Divide your hip measurement into four. Place your clear ruler on the point where your hip measurement stops and draw out another horizontal line to the point where your hip measurement, divided by four, would end.

❑ **Step nine**: take your curved ruler or French curve to join the point you just drew out to connect to the line connecting your hip to your waist point.

❑ **Step ten**: Make your darts by drawing a line from the point of your crotch line divided by four to your waistline. Measure 4 and ½ inches from your waistline down to your hip line. Mark that point on the centerline you have previously drawn. Connect both lines. (An average dart goes 4 and ½ inches down your center front.)

❑ **Step eleven**: divide your thigh measurement, your hip measurement, and draw down.

❑ **Step twelve**: measure the horizontal ankle line and mark it where it ends and the beginning point. Then, use your pattern master to draw from that point up to your thigh line. At this point, you have succeeded in creating most of the front side of your trouser pattern. What is left at this stage is adding your seam allowance and recreating your pattern from the back side.

- ❑ **Step thirteen**: place another pattern paper, or in our case, a dotted paper above your drafted pattern (I prefer a dotted paper because it is lighter and you can easily trace your work into the new paper). Begin to trace your drafted pattern on the new pattern on it. You can use a tracing wheel for this before you begin using a pencil to bold it, or you can go right ahead and use a pencil to trace out what is already done underneath.

- ❑ **Step fourteen**: Mark out the same lines you have made. Cut out excess paper around.

- ❑ **Step fifteen**: Create your seam allowance around it (Standard seam allowance is between half an inch to an inch), depending on what the pattern maker prefers. In my case, I prefer half an inch. You create your seam allowance by measuring out half an inch on all the surrounding areas you have drawn out and adding a parallel line to it. You can cut out more of the excess paper to allow for only your newly-made pattern.

Another way you can replicate your pattern, if you were using a pattern paper, is to place the other pattern paper at the back of it and make it lap properly with a tap. Then you begin to cut through the edges to achieve a second replicate. After this, you can now also use a tracing wheel to achieve the lines and measurements that are on your top pattern paper.

Note that this is a basic fit trouser. If you want to make skinny pants or more fitted trousers, you would have to reduce the width around the thigh to ankle.

That is your basic Male Trouser Pattern! You can now cut out your pattern and cut out the material you want to sew.

Chapter Eight: Project V - Create a Blazer Pattern

Blazers are normally stand-alone clothing, and, most times, you think of a blazer as a jacket that is worn by men and women. A blazer, however, has distinctive features that come with it, and this should be considered when creating or designing a pattern for one. It can be worn over trousers or shorts and would normally come with distinct buttons. Standard blazers have sharp shoulders and come together on the waist area; they drape down a bit close to the crotch level.

Some blazers are made with hard materials like leather, and, in most cases, a lining is also added. All this should be taken into consideration when making your pattern.

Also, the lapels are a very important part of a blazer. Wearing a blazer creates a sort of casual appearance in a normal setting, and it is a nice way to blend into both informal and formal crowds if you are trying to play safe. In this project, we will be creating a blazer.

What you would need

→ Pattern paper

→ A sharp pencil

→ Pattern Master/ Meter ruler

→ Eraser

→ Pen

→ Tracing wheel

→ A basic bodice pattern block

In creating a blazer pattern, we would be working with a basic bodice block to make our blazer pattern. In the previous chapter, we have talked about making a basic bodice block. So you can refer to the preceding chapter to make one. Now, to get started,

- ❑ **Step one**: Spread out your bodice block on another pattern paper that you have spread out on a flat surface.

- ❑ **Step two**: Trace around your basic bodice to create the same block on your new pattern paper. Connect the lines to your waist and sleeves. Add lengths from the waist down if you want your blazer to be longer, which should be the case.

- ❑ **Step three**: Mark one inch out of your waistline. This should be where your button would be placed, depending on the design of your blazer.

- ❑ **Step four**: Draw a line from your line to the hem. Draw the curve from where the arm line is and join it.

- ❑ **Step five**: Make the revere collar- mark half of your back neckline measurement and connect to the front.

- ❑ **Step six**: Mark one inch away from the center front and draw a line.

- ❑ **Step seven**: Add facing and lines for the lining.

- ❑ **Step eight:** Take your newly-completed blazer pattern and place on another clear pattern paper to make the front block of it. After which, you transfer to your material and start stitching.

Chapter Nine:
VI - Ladies' Blouse Pattern and Experimenting with Sleeves

Blouses are an essential part of ladies' clothing. They're worn over skirts and trousers. They have been around for a long time in different styles and forms. One of the essentials of a lady's blouse is the bodice frame, which covers the neckline and the armhole, with all the other upper-body measurements taken into consideration. It should be able to accentuate the waist and the bust, while nicely complementing a skirt or trousers, depending on the design that you are adopting.

A ladies' blouse pattern is much like a basic bodice pattern, which you can now do so much with. In this project, we will be first creating the blouse pattern, after which we will be creating patterns that different sleeves would be added to.

Materials you would need:

→ Set Square

→ Tape measure

→ Pattern master

→ Pattern paper

→ Pencil

To make your blouse pattern, there are some measurements that you should take.

→ The upper bust area

→ The bust line

→ The waistline

→ The hip line

→ The space between the two nipples (for your darts)

❑ **Step one**: Spread out your pattern paper on a flat surface. And make a straight line, or in this case, we would be using the edge of the pattern paper as the centerfold.

❑ **Step two**: Measure out and mark the bustline, the upper bust line, the waistline, and the hip line from the centerfold line (that is the vertical edge of the pattern paper).

❑ **Step three**: Draw out your horizontal lines to the points that you have marked.

❑ **Step four**: Insert your waist darts by dividing your nipple to nipple point measurement into two. Create your darts by drawing a line that starts one inch below the bust line and two inches above the hip line.

❑ **Step five**: Draw out your arm length.

❑ **Step six:** Draw out your neck length and your neck back length.

That is your blouse pattern. Now, we would be following the next steps to create and experiment with a few sleeve patterns on this blouse pattern. There are so many types of sleeves that can be attached to blouses. You can get so many blouse patterns depending on the kind of design that you have created. Here are steps to make a standard sleeve for a blouse.

Take measurements of:

→ Your sleeve length

→ Around your bicep

→ Around your elbow

→ Around the wrist

→ Your arms

❏ **Step one**: Spread out your pattern paper on a flat surface.

❏ **Step two**: Draw a straight line; mark your sleeves length.

❏ **Step three**: Mark your bicep width on the line, mark the elbow, and the wrist width. Join the lines (that is making horizontal lines from the sleeves length).

❏ **Step four:** Mark the midpoint of your bicep width. Draw a line up from the midpoint of your bicep.

❏ **Step five**: Connect the wrist point to the end of the bicep line. Divide the front line slant by four. Mark the points around the slant to make the top sleeve curve.

Your sleeve pattern is normally down for both sides. Even though it can seem complicated, it is so easy, that, when it's done, you can always use it again and again, only making necessary adjustments.

Chapter Ten:
Project VII – Create Six Types of Collar (3 Women and 3 Men)

Collars are a very important part of clothing. In many garments, collars are more than just decoration. Collars found on the neck area of garments both for females and males have now become so important that there are very few garments that don't have one.

Apart from the stylish look they give, collars are also very functional. For instance, they can serve as neck warmers and help reduce cold in chilly parts of the world. It also helps keep the armor from chafing and helps reinforce the neck ends of your fabric to avoid ripping.

There are different kinds of collars. Some can be standing, while others are folded. Irrespective of the type, a standard collar should:

- Embrace the neckline.

- It should be free of any wrinkles.

- It should have smooth curves or sharp points depending on the type or style of the collar.

- It should be interfaced in the right way to retain shape.

- The stitching along the outer seam edge should be stitched in such a way as to make sure that it's not visible.

- The collar should be well-pressed.

- The collar should be graded to reduce thickness.

Basically, you will be creating patterns to conform to the collar you want to make.

Here are the basic kinds of collars for male and female.

For Females, we have:

The Revere Collar: this kind of collar is mostly used for jackets, blazers, or suit jackets. They are normally bigger in size and tend to flatten out at the back; then they merge with a lapel.

Turtle neck Collar: This can be long or short, depending on the style of the design. They are normally standing collars for females, but, overall, in designs today, they are used for both men and women.

Peter Pan Collar: This is a curved flat collar that falls completely on the dress.

Creating Collar patterns

Materials you will need:

→ A sharpened pencil

→ A basic bodice pattern

→ A pattern paper

→ A clear ruler

→ A tracing wheel

→ A measurement of the collar width that you want to make

The Peter Pan Collar

- ❑ **Step one**: Take out the basic bodice pattern and spread on a flat surface. Place another pattern paper under the basic bodice and trace out the back neckline and the armhole.

- ❑ **Step two**: Take your basic bodice front and also place it on the flat surface. Then make your front bodice block and your back bodice block to meet shoulder-to-shoulder. This should form a C- curve. Also, trace out the C-curve, the armhole of the front basic bodice.

- ❑ **Step three**: Use your width measurement to mark points from the end of the neck around the neckline.

- ❑ **Step four**: Make a curve using the points that you have marked.

- ❑ **Step five**: Add another 0.25 cm to hide your seams.

- ❑ **Step six**: Add notches to the front area of your collar.

- ❑ **Step seven**: Cut out your pattern to begin sewing.

The Turtle Neck Collar

- ❑ **Step one**: Take out the basic bodice pattern and spread it on a flat surface. Place another pattern paper under the basic bodice and trace out the back neckline and the armhole.

- ❑ **Step two**: Take your basic bodice front and also place it on the flat surface. Use your width measurement to mark points from the end of your neck to how high you want your turtle neck to get to.

- ❏ **Step three**: Draw the line from your neck curve to meet the point you have marked.

- ❏ **Step four**: Use your curved ruler to curve the end of the neckline connecting to the newly ruled line so as to make a curve.

- ❏ **Step five**: Add another 0.25 cm to hide your seams.

- ❏ **Step six**: Add notches to the front area of your collar.

- ❏ **Step seven**: cut out your pattern to begin sewing.

The Revere Collar

- ❏ **Step one**: Take out the basic bodice pattern and spread it on a flat surface. Place another pattern paper under the basic bodice and trace out the back neckline and the armhole.

- ❏ **Step two**: First, design your lapel by marking the lines in front of the bodice length.

- ❏ **Step three:** Take your basic bodice front and also place it on the flat surface. Mark a line on top of your neckline; that would join your neckline to make your reverse collar.

For males, we have:

The Open Sport Collar

The open sport collar is normally for a man's sport shirt. These shirts are mostly buttoned up.

- ❑ **Step one**: Take out the basic bodice pattern and spread it on a flat surface. Place another pattern paper under the basic bodice and trace out the back neckline and the armhole.

- ❑ **Step two**: First, design your lapel by marking the lines in front of the bodice length.

- ❑ **Step three**: Take your basic bodice front and also place it on the flat surface. Mark a line on top of your neckline; that would join your neckline to make your sports collar.

The Mandarin Collar

The mandarin collar sits around the neck on formal men's clothing. Follow these steps to draft the collar.

- ❑ **Step one:** Take out the basic bodice pattern and spread it on a flat surface. Place another pattern paper under the basic bodice and trace out the back neckline.

- ❑ **Step two**: Measure and mark out the points of the mandarin collar. If you want it standard, you should ensure that you measure just one inch. If you want it longer, you should increase it by half an inch higher.

- ❑ **Step three:** Mark the seam allowances on your neckline. Measure from the center back to the shoulder line. Then measure from the centre front to the front shoulder line.

- ❑ **Step four**: Connect the points you have marked, and draw your lines to connect from the beginning of center back and the center front to the measured area.

- ❑ **Step five:** Add ¼ inch around the lines connected to form your seam lines and cut out your mandarin collar pattern.

The Square Collar

To draft the square collar, follow the steps below,

- ❏ **Step one**: Take out the basic bodice pattern and spread it on a flat surface. Place another pattern paper under the basic bodice and trace out the back neckline.

- ❏ **Step two**: Measure and mark out the points of the square collar.

- ❏ **Step three**: Mark the seam allowances on your neckline. Measure from the center back to the shoulder line. Then, measure from the center front to the front shoulder line.

- ❏ **Step four**: Connect the points you have marked, and draw your lines to connect from the beginning of center back and the center front to the measured area.

- ❏ **Step five**: Cut out the square Collar Pattern.

Once they're created, you can easily fit your collars on your neckline. Collars continue to be an irreplaceable aspect of most clothing.

Conclusion

Pattern making is a very important aspect of apparel design, fitting, and alterations. You can do nothing of significance without these attributes. Great pattern-makers become so with years of experience and usually continue to teach others.

In this guide, we have established that, with diligence and great eye for detail, there's nothing stopping you from creating some of the world's best designs. The only ceiling is your imagination and creativity.

Even though there are so many beautiful designs today, why shouldn't the future be draped with inventions that only you can imagine?

We have also established that understanding the fundamentals will guide you into making the right choices. You'll learn the right way to design and make alterations for the best fit.

Those who have done it in the past, and have laid the groundwork for us today, discovered that apparel designing was not just their career but their vocation.

Some famous pattern designers include:

Alexander McQueen

Alexander Mcqueen was the chief fashion designer at Givenchy from 1996 to 2012, after which he started his label. He became one of the major designers of the 21st Century and has made his mark in the fashion industry with his work in Givenchy. He was very innovative, often disruptive, and continued to break rules and present new ideas. He designed the armadillo heels and the low waisted trend of the time. Some critics even called him the hooligan of fashion as he continued to create over-the-top designs. His designs were also notable for their precision and detailed touch.

He often draped on models and started from the side to cut. According to him, this was to ensure that all the curves and lumps were dealt with precisely, and nothing was missed out. One of his other notable designs recently is the Misses/Misses' petite jumpsuit. This is loose on the waist, straight-legged, has shoulder pads, a side zip, and side buttons. This pattern was embraced by professional and home sewers alike. His collections also carried lots of silhouettes. His approach has featured wide neck dresses with a combination of different fabrics to transcend trends.

Stella McCartney

The daughter of one of the world-famous Beatles, Stella McCartney is an English fashion designer. She has continued to impress the world of fashion since 1995. Her clean-cut garments continue to give her an edge, especially when it comes to women's wear, from everyday clothes to dinner apparel. She has designed ladies' bags, sneakers, and jewelry. She campaigns for animal rights; her clothes are not made with fur or leather. Her best pieces are feminine, comfortable, and sharp. Her styles range from ankle cut pants to blazers and coats. She loves to use bright colors and soft fabrics.

Phoebe Philio

Former creative director of Celine, Phoebe Philio has been a big name in the fashion industry. Her designs are a reflection of her Northern English heritage since she focuses on designs for working-class women; clothes that are chic, classy, and comfortable. Phoebe's work is suitable for office apparel and an evening out.

Alexander Wang

Alexander Wang is one of the major designers in fashion today. His styles are embraced by both old and young. They are mostly ready-to-wear, plus comfortable women's and men's wear. His shirt-like design that forms a skirt that buttons down while the sleeves tie in front is especially chic and fun. His 2015 winter collection also broke boundaries with unusual button positions and spiraling zippers. Classic tailoring pieces were reinvented to have the crotch area redesigned to the back, and included top-stitched shaped pockets. His designs have reinvented female wear and have been resonant, comfortably competing with some of the big names of fashion.

Marc Jobs

Marc Jacob is an American fashion designer who became prominent after designing men's wear and swimwear for years under his own brand. He has created styles that have stormed the red carpet; they've adorned numerous celebrities. He is known for mixing some street-wise aesthetics to his designs, which makes them appealing to young people.

Tom Ford

Tom Ford is a notable designer who has previously been creative fashion director at Gucci and Yves Saint Laurent. He is well known for his men's suit designs, and has notably designed for celebrities and politicians. Names like Michelle Obama, Justine Timberlake, and Beyonce are on his list. He brings a powerful sensual look to his style. He has designs ranging from men's wear, jewelry, and women's wear. He is also a well-regarded film director.

Christain Louboutin

Christain Louboutin is best known for his works with shoes. He says that entertainment was a strong inspiration for him, and one of his greatest fascinations was ladies dancing in high heels. Understanding them was understanding how women wanted their shoes to be. Whenever you see glossy red stiletto shoes, you know it may well be a Louboutin design.

Today the world is fast-paced, and while you can still make the best designs manually, there is also great pattern-making software available that makes the work very easy for you. With the use of such software, you can save time, energy, and resources. No need for the clutter that comes with cutting and gluing when you can do all that on a screen. You can easily store them in your device and make alterations and as many designs as you want for future use. They are quite flexible, and you do not have to be an expert to use them. The higher-range ones are a bit pricey, but they may be something to consider.

Here are some important and affordable pattern softwares that you should check out;

Computer-Aided Design Software: Softwares like Optitex, Gerber, Lectra are great for pattern makers and sewers. This software allows you to transform simple sketches to digital illustration, also making it easy to add measurements and grade patterns. It comes with a 2D and 3D effect.

Wild Things: This is another great software that helps you creatively draw and illustrate your designs, it also allows you to print them out, and it comes with a guide to give you step-by-step actions on how to use it. It also comes with a feature that helps you create embellishment and accessories for your design. And it's free!

Inkscape: This is a great professional drafting software. It allows you to draft patterns easily and can be used in 2D and 3D drawings. It is strictly for pattern drafting and works well in using shapes, objects, and freehand drawing to design your patterns.

GIMP: This is an excellent pattern making and sewing tool. It comes with a full package to draft and create designs and also to produce them. It allows you to integrate with other software tools and also offers features that help you to retouch and remake your designs quickly. It provides different file formats to save your documents and also comes with good tutorials.

More and more software tools will be created to help make fashion much easier, especially when it comes to design. Regardless, the fundamentals remain the same and will always be there to guide you to make good choices.

As the world continues to evolve, apparel designs have come and gone. There are some designs that have come and have remained constant while others become yesterday's trends. Historically, people would first think of body presentation and the need to conform to culture, social class, and moral standards. In today's world, creativity and comfort have become one of the major factors of design. We see it from long straight skirts to short skirts. There have been some great apparel designs over the years that have stood the test of time. These designs have remained relevant and continue to transcend passing fads.

The palazzo trousers: The palazzo trousers have been fashionable for a long time; they are quite comfortable and airy. They sit well on the female form and can be worn both formally and casually, depending on the design and fit. They normally hold the waist and drape down to the ankles and can be worn with pumps.

The Spanx: What would the ladies do without a pair of spanx? This apparel is a much-needed shapewear that has continued to be a favorite item in every woman's wardrobe.

Denim jeans: These are apparel designs that have been around for a long time. There is something about their comfort and fit that brings a casual balance to everything.

These designs continue to rock the world, and, most of the time, are redefined to be used again and again. From the straight skirt to a simple tee-shirt to a complicated ball gown by Alexander McQueen, fitting the form remains paramount. Hence, pattern fitting and alteration in fashion design is not a master to itself or apart from the individual. It is worthy of note that no matter how great a design might be, without a person to wear it, it is no more than useless. The goal remains fitting the form and highlighting its best assets while providing great comfort.

As a fashion student, this tells you that there is still much more to be done, and you are only a pencil and paper away from creating a new design that might amaze everyone. We can see that the world's best designers have one thing in common; they choose to push boundaries but also stick to the fundamentals. One area that was highlighted throughout this guide is the importance of understanding the fundamentals and basics. If you remember this, you will go far in your own journey of innovation.